MY TIME AMONG THE WHITES

MY TIME AMONG THE WHITES

Notes from an Unfinished Education

JENNINE
CAPÓ
CRUCET

PICADOR

ST. MARTIN'S PRESS | NEW YORK

MY TIME AMONG THE WHITES. Copyright © 2019 by Jennine Capó Crucet. All rights reserved. Printed in the United States of America. For information, address Picador, 120 Broadway, New York, N.Y. 10271.

picadorusa.com · instagram.com/picador
twitter.com/picadorusa · facebook.com/picadorusa

Picador® is a U.S. registered trademark and is used by Macmillan Publishing Group, LLC, under license from Pan Books Limited.

For book club information, please visit facebook.com/picadorbookclub or email marketing@picadorusa.com.

Portions of the essays in this collection originally appeared, in different form, in the following publications: "A Prognosis" in *Medium* and *Gay Magazine*; "What We Pack," "Say I Do," "Going Cowboy," "A Prognosis," "Ease of Exit," and "The Country We Now Call Home" in *The New York Times*.

Designed by Richard Oriolo

The Library of Congress Cataloging-in-Publication Data is available upon request.

ISBN 9781250299437 (trade paperback) | ISBN 9781250299444 (ebook)

Our books may be purchased in bulk for promotional, educational, or business use. Please contact your local bookseller or the Macmillan Corporate and Premium Sales Department at 1-800-221-7945, extension 5442, or by email at MacmillanSpecialMarkets@macmillan.com.

First Edition: September 2019

10 9 8 7 6 5 4 3 2 1

For my parents, who made everything possible,
and for Palomita

CONTENTS

I

EARLY
ENCOUNTERS

WHAT WE PACK

T WAS A SIMPLE QUESTION, BUT WE COULDN'T find the answer in any of the paperwork the college had sent: How long was my family supposed to stay for first-year student orientation? This may seem easy enough to answer now, but this was 1999 and Google wasn't yet a verb, and we were a low-income family (according to my new school) without regular internet access. I was the first in my family to go to college, which made me a first-generation college student as well as a first-generation American, because my parents were born in Cuba. We didn't know that families were supposed to leave campus almost immediately after they unloaded your stuff from the car.

Together we made the trip from my hometown of Miami to what would be my new college home in upstate New York. Shortly after arriving on campus, the five of us—both of my parents, my younger sister, my abuela, and me—found ourselves listening to a dean end his welcome speech with the words: "Now, parents, please, go. Your child is in good hands. Time to cut the cord. Go home."

Almost everyone in the audience laughed, but not me, and not my parents. They turned to me and said, "What does he mean, *go*?" My abuela asked my sister in Spanish, "What? What's he saying?" a new note of panic in her voice because my sister had stopped translating. She didn't know how, exactly, to translate the dean's joke. She turned to me like something was my fault and said, "But orientation's just started." I was just as confused as they were. We thought we *all* needed to be there for first-year orientation—the whole family, for the whole week. My dad had booked their hotel room until the day after my classes officially began. They'd used all their vacation time from work and had been saving for months to get me to school and go through what we'd thought of as *our* orientation.

This confusion isn't the most common or problematic issue first-generation college students and their families face—not by a long shot—but it shows just how clueless and out of our element we were. Another example: Every afternoon during that week, we had to go back to the only department store we could find, the now defunct Ames, for some stupid thing we hadn't known was a necessity, something not in our budget, things like shower shoes, a bathrobe, a plastic soap holder (we hadn't realized the bathroom situation would be a communal one—in fact, we hadn't thought about the bathroom situation *at all*), extra-long twin sheets, mesh laundry bags. Before the other families left, we carefully watched them because they looked at ease, like they knew what they were doing, and we made new shopping lists with our limited vocabulary: *Those things that lift up the bed*, we wrote. *That plastic thing to carry stuff to the bathroom.*

My family followed me around as I visited department offices during course registration. "Only four classes?" they asked, assuming I was mistakenly taking my first semester too easy. And I'd agreed: Like most high schoolers, I'd taken six classes every year, so four seemed like nothing—this kind of assumption being one of the more common first-generation college student mistakes, one I thankfully didn't make.

They went with me to the campus store to buy my books, and together we learned what the stickers on worn copies promised: Used Saves. They walked me to orientation events they thought they'd also be attending and to buildings I was supposed to be finding on my own. They waited outside those buildings so that we could all leave from there and go to lunch together. The five of us wandered each day through the dining hall's doors. "You guys are still here!" the over-friendly person swiping ID cards said after day three. "They sure are!" I chirped back, learning via the cues of my hallmates that I was supposed to want my family gone. But it was an act: I wanted them there. We sat together at meals—amid all the other students, already making friends—my mom placing a napkin and fork at each seat, setting the table as we did at home.

I don't remember the moment they drove away. I'm told it's one of those instances you never forget, that second when you realize you're finally on your own, a feeling of fear mixed with freedom, and also, I'm told, with relief. But for me, the memory of that moment just doesn't exist—perhaps because, when you're the first in your family to go to college, you never truly feel like you're there on your own.

■

I'd applied to only two places for college, the University of Florida and Cornell University, because applying to college was (and is) an expensive process, and I didn't know about fee waivers. My decision to apply specifically to Cornell—a choice that would eventually change the course of my life—might as well have occurred randomly. I was waiting in a high school guidance counselor's office for a schedule change as she silently sorted through a pile of college-related junk mail (she wasn't the college counselor, and that year, as far as I knew, my high school didn't have one). When I saw a cover image flash by—that of a tree bursting red with color, in the height of its fall foliage—I blurted out, "What's that one?" and lurched forward to put my hand on top of it, to stop her sorting. She handed it to me as an afterthought, without even looking up, and the rest of the brochures—all these other possible versions of my future—went into her recycling bin. I learned from that viewbook that Cornell was the first of the Ivy League schools to admit women and people of color. I thought that was cool, and that was enough to make me want to try and get accepted (but not necessarily go). This single experience, coming before easy access to the internet, constituted the bulk of my college research process. There was a paper application inside that viewbook, which I would eventually fill out and send off with all the other pieces of information Cornell required, including an application fee.

By some measures, most of them financial, my choice to attend Cornell was not a smart one. And when I say "my," I mean "me and my entire family," because the decision never felt wholly my own to make, as I understood that my choice would impact my parents' lives in drastic ways none of us could fully anticipate. What I did know was that, thanks to my good grades and various state initiatives meant to entice

7

students to stay in the state for college, I had an excellent financial aid package from the University of Florida (UF): full tuition, room and board covered, the additional scholarships I'd earned through other channels all landing in my pocket to cover books and other expenses. I could afford to have a car. I could come home on weekends if I wanted. I was about to be the first in my family to go to college, and it wouldn't cost us a cent. Thanks to rolling admissions, I knew by October that I'd been admitted, and by November, I was stockpiling Gator paraphernalia.

Then, in April, I got into Cornell. I now know that their financial aid package was also strong, but it didn't feel that way then: There was a subsidized loan of four thousand a year that was in my name, and in addition to that, there was an "expected family contribution" (or EFC) of a few thousand dollars—a gap in my aid package that my parents were expected to cover and that could (and would) change each year.

The questions for us became: Did I *need* to go to the more expensive school? Would it really make a tangible difference in my life?

I had the privilege of supportive parents who, while they definitely wanted me closer to home, had been convinced by both me and the school trying to recruit me that going to Cornell was an investment in a future that—though we couldn't quite picture it—we somehow intuited we'd be foolish to pass up. We didn't know what exactly we were investing in, only that the result of this investment was whoever I was going to be. I look back on it now and cannot believe what I did to my parents: They remortgaged their home, which they'd already paid off (hence the financial aid office seeing it as a resource they could tap) to cover what Cornell calculated they could afford.

Recently I called my mom in Miami to ask her why in the end they agreed to let me turn down a free ride to UF.

"Don't you remember?" she said. "We went to that Cornell recruitment thing at that man's house in Coral Gables. He was a lawyer or something. Me and your father couldn't sleep that night. We were talking, thinking, okay, we're two stupid people—not stupid, you know what I mean—and these people, they were just . . . we wanted that for you, for you to have all that, be all that."

"But isn't that wrong, the way that event made you feel? Wasn't that manipulative?"

"Of course it was! That's how the world works! You know that," she said.

I only remember the inside of that house in Coral Gables (which is one of the Miami area's wealthiest neighborhoods, and which is in fact its own city). The host had a whole room in his house just for his family's books—a room I now know is called a study—and jutting out from one of the built-in bookshelves was a desk, and on top of that was the family's computer. He'd used the internet to pull up that morning's issue of *The Cornell Daily Sun*, the campus newspaper. He'd let me sit at the desk and read it while the rest of the house hummed with laughing and talking. And floating just under the talking, classical music, which emanated from speakers I couldn't see, only feel. I remember looking around, trying and failing to find them.

I couldn't understand back then that attending Cornell would plug me into a kind of access and privilege I didn't yet have a name for. But my parents, having worked trade jobs their whole lives, knew better.

My mother said, "Do you really think you'd be where you are now if you'd gone to UF?"

I can't say where I'd be had I not asked a bored counselor to hand me a brochure she was about to throw away. All I can possibly know is where I am now, which is far from home, living dependent-free, in a landlocked state, writing books and working as a newly tenured professor at a Big Ten school in a city where I am related to absolutely no one. My best friend from high school, who graduated second in our class and was supposed to be my Gator roommate, went to UF and loved it. She finished a semester early, married her high school boyfriend, and has two gorgeous children and an amazing house. She has rewarding friendships (she's substituted me as her BFF with a woman whose life on Instagram looks equally amazing—by which I mean she seems to own a boat). She has a fulfilling career. She has a loving relationship with her parents and sees them all the time.

There is no "but" here.

■

At Cornell, the woman in the dorm room next to mine was from Iowa, from a family of pig farmers; she'd almost gone to the University of Iowa instead of Cornell. She ended up transferring there after our first year. As she put it, she just didn't need Cornell (and its accompanying price tag) for what she wanted to do with her future, though I'm sure there was more to it than that. The girls in my hall—myself included, all of us from the East Coast—teased her mercilessly for being from Iowa and for coming from a pig farming background, behavior of which I am now ashamed. (At the Lincoln farmers' market, there is always a vendor selling a T-shirt that says IOWA HAS BAD CORN, and I think that might be the meanest it gets out here when it comes to teasing people from Iowa. Also, the irony of the fact that I recently needed to take a class in Omaha on half-hog butchery—to write a compelling, believable scene for a new short story set in Miami—just to learn things my former hallmate likely came to college already knowing is not lost on me.) A year away showed her what she actually needed from her college experience, and when she chose to transfer, I couldn't help but think she'd outsmarted a system into which I'd naively fallen without a firm sense of what to expect or demand from it.

What I still find remarkable is that a decision I made at seventeen, with very little information or guidance, has gone on to shape my entire life. Maybe this feels remarkable to me because it's a lasting characteristic of the first-gen college student identity, which can carry with it the knowledge of a shadow life, one where you're equally happy having done something or gone somewhere else. Or maybe the decision still feels astonishing to me because I initially chose to attend a completely different university, its two biggest draws being that it was essentially free and that my best friend would be there—two reasons that seemed good to me and to my family, in part because none of us knew what we could or should expect from the college experience. Perhaps what needs the most consideration when college commitments are being made is not which college, but what you feel you need from a school, and that's a tricky set of qualities to recognize (and an even trickier thing to trust) when you're the first in your family to set off down that path. When I walked around UF's campus, a visit I made with my mom after having already tentatively committed to the school, I didn't feel anything, except some vague unease. I couldn't explain it, and I'm glad I didn't rationalize it away. I'm glad my parents didn't ask me to try to articulate what, exactly, felt wrong for me about the place. They were teaching me to trust my gut.

I don't know why UF didn't feel like the right college home for me, but that feeling was strong enough to make me sign on for some major financial commitments at a school more than a thousand miles away at the ripe old age of eighteen, a school that may not have been right for me either, but which felt more right than my other option. I want to be clear: Debt was not something I took on lightly, and it would probably be harder for me to make the same decision today that I made in 1999, with the amount of debt feeling even more insurmountable because of fears about what the job market would look like when I finished. And excellent opportunities abound at public universities across the United States (I teach at one now, and I have amazing students who I know will go on to change the world). But at that Cornell recruitment reception, there was this vague promise being held out to me, to my family—not just of economic opportunity, but of the opportunity to transcend the limits of my imagination about who I might someday be. But only the economic one was visible from the minute we drove into that neighborhood to meet other students admitted to Cornell, many of them from private high schools, many of them seeing the financial aid as irrelevant to their decision: They'd be paying most if not all of the cost anywhere they went. For them, whatever came next was worth that cost, and *that* was the promise my family and I could recognize and want for ourselves.

A promise is not the same as a guarantee, but we couldn't yet tell the difference.

■

When I started high school, my mother took me to the orthodontist. I had inherited my parents' jacked-up teeth, and at the time when most of my friends were getting their braces removed, we were there to potentially *start* the whole ordeal, finally in an economic position that let us take on the debt of braces. After poking around in my mouth and taking impressions of my teeth, the orthodontist declared that I did not *need* braces—my bite was a little off but mostly fine, so braces weren't necessary; they'd be purely for cosmetic reasons.

Because we'd already identified ourselves as the kind of people who would need help affording orthodontics, the doctor thought this news would come as a relief to my mother. It did not. She started crying, and I was confused. (I was fourteen and happy to hear I could dodge the discomfort my friends had endured.)

"If she needed them, it would be easier in my head to pay for it," she said. "Everyone is getting braces, someday they'll all be people with straight teeth. I don't want her to have crooked teeth when she's thirty." She pointed toward her own mouth.

My mother wanted to give me an advantage she never had, and this desire in and of itself counts as a need. Yes, it was rooted in unfairness—in her knowledge that people would make assumptions about me based on something superficial—but it was too deep in her gut to ignore. She needed to be someone who could give her daughter this gift.

I should mention that my mother has a beautiful, almost perfect smile. Her own braces came as an adult, after a car accident pushed all her teeth in. I never really noticed they were still a little crooked, though now that we live far from each other, it's something that, when I first see her after months apart, I can't help but notice.

My braces came off my junior year. I am in my thirties now and still sometimes wear my top retainer: I grind my teeth in my sleep, unconsciously undoing the work of making them straight. The bottom retainer no longer fits at all because I lost it for a couple of years, and when I found it in a move and went to pop it in, my teeth had already shifted too much, perhaps because of the wisdom tooth still in my lower jaw (though I hear that's a myth), or maybe the nail biting I can't curtail, or perhaps just time. In fact, my bottom teeth are almost back to where they started despite those braces. What a waste of all that metal, that pain, and that work. With that gift came the commitment to honor and maintain it, and perhaps because I was the first in my family to have such a gift, I didn't know that things never stop shifting, that getting the chance at something better doesn't automatically guarantee it.

■

A couple of weeks into my first semester of classes at Cornell, after my parents finally abandoned me far above Cayuga's waters, I received the topics for what would be my first college paper, in an English course on the modern novel. I might as well have been my abuela trying to read and understand them; the language felt that foreign. I called my mom at work and in tears told her that I had to come home, that I'd made a terrible mistake, that I should've gone to UF, where everyone seemed to be having a lot more fun than I was.

She sighed into the phone. I heard the chatter of her two-way radio behind her, electricians asking questions about permits and supply deliveries, asking my mom (who the workers called Base, since she worked from an office) for updates. She turned down the volume and said, "Just read me the first question. We'll go through it a little at a time and figure it out."

I read her the topics slowly, pausing after each sentence, waiting for her to say something, just an *mmhmm* or the conversational throw-me-a-bone of *okay*. The first topic was two paragraphs long. I remember it had the word *intersectionalities* in it. And the word *gendered*. I waited for her response and for the ways it would encourage me, for her to tell me I could do this, but I knew from my mother's total silence that, like me, she'd never before heard these words: my first insight into how access to certain vocabularies was a kind of privilege.

Of course, I didn't know to call this *privilege*, not yet.

"You're right," my mother said after a moment. "You're screwed."

Parents who've gone to college themselves know that at this point they should encourage their kid to go to office hours, or to the writing center, or to ask the professor or a TA for clarification—that it's not just a student's right but their responsibility as budding scholars to do so. But my mom thought I was as on my own as I feared. While my college had done an excellent job recruiting me, I had no blueprint or road map for what I was supposed to do once I made it to campus, how I was going to spend the next four years. I'd already embarrassed myself by doing things like asking my RA what time the dorm closed for the night. As far as I knew, there'd been no mandatory meeting geared toward first-generation students like me. Aside from a check-in with my financial aid officer, where she explained what work-study was (I didn't know and worried it meant I had to join the army or something) and where she had me sign for my loan, I'd been mostly keeping to myself to hide the fact that I was a very special kind of lost: What seemed obvious to many students left me flailing. This was a feeling shared by my parents, who had no idea what they were supposed to say, who couldn't suggest I just come home for the weekend, and who didn't know to offer solutions that seemed obvious to people who've been to college themselves. This, too, is a kind of privilege: the resource of people—people who love you—who have navigated a version of the very system you are now navigating.

"I mean, I literally have no idea what any of that means," my mom said. "I don't even know how it's a *question.*"

I folded the sheet with the paper topics in half and put it in my desk drawer.

"I don't know what you're gonna do," my mom almost laughed. "Maybe—have you looked in the dictionary?"

I started crying harder, my hand over the receiver.

"You still there?" she eventually asked.

I murmured, "*Mmhmm.*"

"Look, just stick it out up there until Christmas," she said. "We have no more vacation days this year. We can't take off any more time to go get you."

"Okay," I swallowed (my OK having that sharp *a*, a still present relic of my Miami accent that only *okay*, on the page, accurately represents). I started breathing in through my nose and out through my mouth, calming myself. "I can do that," I said.

My mom laughed for real this time and said, "Mamita, you don't really have a choice."

She didn't say this in a mean way. She was just telling me the truth. "This whole thing was your idea, remember?"

It sounded almost like a threat—and there it was: the beginning of a kind of resentment many first-generation college students come to know, one born from our families' frustrations at no longer knowing how to help us. Yes, it had been my idea. I'd argued with them that going away to Cornell would be the best thing for the whole family in the long run, but none of us could predict how vast the distance would come to feel, how it would move me into a different class of people— out of the class that had forged me—and that this shift would remain a painful source of tension from that moment on.

The racket of radios started up again—so much static

and screaming—and my mom told me she had to go, that she needed to get back to work.

So I got back to work, too, and *Get back to work* became a sort of mantra for me. I tackled the paper with the same focus that had landed me at Cornell in the first place. I did okay on it, earning a B-/C (I never found out how a grade could have a slash in it, but now that I'm an English professor I understand perfectly what he meant with that grade). The professor had covered the typed pages with handwritten comments and questions, which I took as a bad thing rather than as a sign of his engagement with my work and the kind of attention my tuition dollars were affording me, and so I never followed up with him about my paper as I should have. It was in his endnote (the first one I had ever received in my academic career, looking like its own small essay) where he listed the various campus resources available to me—the writing center, his office hours—that I first learned of their existence.

My mom didn't ask outright what grade I earned on the paper. She eventually stopped asking about assignments altogether. And I learned from my peers that grades were something I didn't have to share with my parents the way I had in high school. My report card had transformed into a *transcript*, a euphemism I'd deploy in December when my mom asked when my school would be sending her the former.

My grades were the first of many elements of my new life for which they had no context. With each passing semester, what I was doing became, for them, as indecipherable as that paper topic. They didn't even know what questions to ask, which is also the quintessential condition of the first-generation college student experience—though I wouldn't begin to understand this until long after I'd earned my degree. The question my parents were really asking when they wondered if I "needed" to go to the more expensive school was: Which option has the potential to open the most doors, and how much can we afford to hope she'll walk through them? It's a more complex question. And they knew more than I did that there wasn't a straightforward answer, in part because of the word *potential*, which acknowledges the lack of guarantees, and in part because the answer depended on what I'd make out of whichever version of my education we bought into. My college education eventually taught me to pursue harder, more complex questions, that asking harder questions is one of the most important things a person can do. I was learning, with each seemingly more baffling paper topic, how to think critically—a skill I use on itself, to ask whether or not I could've learned it just as thoroughly without going into debt.

My parents know for a fact that going to the more expensive school was the best investment they ever made in me. But I can admit that I'll never know for sure. And I know enough to recognize my ambivalence as a sign that perhaps proves them right.

¡NOTHING IS IMPOSSIBLE
IN AMERICA!

WHEN NON-LATINX AMERICANS MEET ME AND learn my family is from Cuba, they often ask me one of two bizarre questions. The first is if I've ever been to Cuba, a question so layered and fraught for me that I've learned to respond by asking, "Why would I have ever been to Cuba?" and then just seeing what they say. I almost relish their awkward answers and the assumptions they reveal.

I got this question a lot when I lived in Minnesota, a place where many of my students bragged about their Scandinavian heritage, and it never once occurred to me to ask, within seconds of meeting them, if they'd ever been to Sweden.

The second question, less common though still fairly fraught, isn't even actually a question: Oh, that's weird/interesting/funny, they say, *Jennine* isn't a very Cuban name.

You are correct, I say. It is not.

I often want to fill the uncomfortable pause that follows with a story about the American Dream that goes like this: Two kids from Cuba meet as teenagers in Carol City, Florida. They have names—given to them by Cuban parents who mistakenly assumed that they'd live in Cuba pretty much forever—that mark them as ethnic minorities in the United States. These names, in their new home country, impact everything about their lives: their educations (and the premature ends of those educations), their job prospects, in what areas of the city they can look for a home. They marry young, start a family young. Because they are light-skinned they reason that there's a chance their American-born offspring could avoid at least some elements of the systemic prejudice they encountered (despite having worked hard to learn English and almost eradicating their accents—this is, after all, a story about the American Dream, right? Which means that many things will need to be unjustly eradicated). In this version of the American Dream, they think that all it takes to change your destiny in this country is picking the right name for your child.

They are not totally wrong. As John Oliver (on his show *Last Week Tonight*) pointed out when, in his pre-election efforts to "Make Donald Drumpf Again," he told a (possibly apocryphal) story about the then candidate's grandfather, saying he'd changed the family last name from Drumpf to Trump when he emigrated from Germany. Oliver asked viewers, specifically those thinking of voting for the man, to "stop and take a moment to imagine how you would feel if you just met a guy named Donald Drumpf." It's a joke that plays on xenophobia, and Oliver is only pointing out a reality for many Americans—a reality the couple in the above story had lived through and saw an opportunity to alter for (what they hoped was) the better.

Because of the experience of living with their own names, my parents thought that giving their American child a distinctly ethnic name came with unfair, quantifiable consequences— they sensed this long before research studies would show which names on similar résumés got to count as qualified for a job— and having weathered those consequences themselves, they felt an understandable reluctance to have me inherit them.

This is how I came to be named after the 1980 Miss USA runner-up. My parents had a loose plan to name me after the winner, and they had settled into bed on a May evening to watch the pageant with that intention, even though I wouldn't be born until July 1981 (they've always been the type to plan ahead). I was to be not just their first kid but also the first born-in-America American in our family. Perhaps they felt a suitable American name was needed to commemorate this leap from Cubans to Americans. Should I happen to be born female, what better place to find that name, they thought, than an American beauty pageant?

Bob Barker played host back then, and they must've liked the way the name sounded in his *Price Is Right* drawl. Yes, the man who made his living encouraging people to spin a giant wheel and asking them how much they thought random crap was worth (without overestimating!) helped determine the proper noun that would identify me for the rest of my life. I imagine that long skinny microphone topped with that perfect black ball, no harsh consonants to pop or *s*'s to hiss—*jeh-neeeeeen*—his pointy white teeth seizing that second syllable like a cartoon cat catching a mouse by the tail.

Although my parents—their names are Maria and Evaristo—were rooting for her, Jineane Ford aka Miss Arizona didn't win. The winner of the 1980 Miss USA pageant, the person after whom I was supposed to be named, was Shawn Weatherly, that year's Miss South Carolina. I can almost hear my parents deciding, their pact to name me after the winner be damned, that Shawn was a boy's name despite evidence to the contrary standing right in front of them, wearing a crown.

So, close enough, there was my name: Jineane. But that *spelling*, they thought. Their Spanish-language origins got the better of them and they agreed this spelling was all wrong, the vowels in her name making little sense, that early *i* right after the *j* reading and sounding like *ee* to them. Let's change that to an *e*. And while we're at it, let's keep customizing: Change the original *e* to an *i*, throw an extra *n* before that for (I guess?) balance, lose the *a*—what is that *ah* sound doing in there anyway?—but let's keep that last *e* because in English people always put a silent *e* on the end, right? Jennine. Daughter named! They had no idea that in altering the spelling they were undoing the work of making the name something that would help me pass: Although I'm sure the *sound* of it has opened doors that might've otherwise been unfairly closed, when seen in writing, the spelling always flags for certain people—people looking for it—as a marker of my parents' immigrant status, their alterations betraying the reason they went with that name in the first place.

The first real short story I ever wrote as a college student for a fiction workshop tried to explore this moment between them, the negotiation of it. In it, a nineteen-year-old woman and her husband of almost two years are discussing what to name their baby if it's a girl. The husband is confident it will be a boy. The woman decides to stake the name on a televised beauty pageant, one she's never seen, and they proceed to watch it together, the woman feeling predictably huge at the sight of so many skinny white women floating across the stage. At some point the husband brings her a sandwich. He is used to having *her* bring *him* sandwiches, but she can't get off of the couch. They very subtly bring up the racism they encounter because of their own markedly Spanish names. (One workshop critique from my all-white college classmates was that they didn't think the scene was "loud enough" and wanted this conversation between the couple to be more explicit, their assumption being that people of color regularly sit around discussing their oppression outright as they watch TV at home.) They bet on their kid being light-skinned enough to eventually pass as white and decide they should give her a name that encourages her to do so. The winner's name in the short story is Paige, which neither parent can pronounce correctly, and which doesn't work in Spanish at all, so they go with Sandra, the name of a contestant who finished in the top ten but scored highest in the interview portion. The story ends with both characters burping, thus beginning my obsession with bodily functions as significant gestures in fiction.

It wasn't a great story, but it showed promise—at least enough to garner my professor's attention and encouragement, which is sometimes all a budding writer needs. I told no one in class that the story was based on how I got my name, even when they discussed how improbable the scenario seemed to them, how pointedly symbolic it was, how totally unlikely it would be—these white classmates told me—for a Cuban couple not to want to honor their own heritage in the naming of their first child.

Okay.

Truth be told, part of me agreed with my classmates, and I never fully believed this was how my parents chose my name until college, when I looked up the pageant's results, prompted by the workshop assignment, and learned, horrified, that my name's origin story was a real fact of my life. What were my parents aiming for, naming me after a beauty queen? What were they trying to say about the kind of daughter they wanted? What were they hoping for—wishing for me, willing me to be—with this name?

Or was it more about what they were trying to prove to the country that had taken them in as children? Perhaps their idea was more in line with names like Usnavy and Usmarine—the names Cuban refugees sometimes give their newborn American children as homage to the first words they saw upon arrival or rescue: U.S. Navy, U.S. Marine. Our names: a form of gratitude, or of allegiance, and in my case, a kind of skin-deep hope.

■

Who is this woman, Jineane Ford, the beauty queen after whom I was named, whose parents got just as creative with the vowels? Jineane Ford, born the same year as my mother, 1960, from Gilbert, Arizona. She allegedly tripped during the evening wear portion of the competition and hit the ground in view of Bob Barker. Perhaps this is what endeared her to my parents: that she could mess up so royally (pun intended) but still manage to finish (almost) on top. That she could play off what should've been a disaster—after all, the only real directive in the evening wear competition is WALK ACROSS THE STAGE WITHOUT FALLING—as something charming. Maybe they liked that she was resilient, tough, not easily embarrassed. Very American. And she didn't take herself too seriously; maybe they would've named me after her even if she'd finished dead last. In my more generous moments, I let myself believe this.

■

The American Dream, commonly told: You can accomplish anything if you work hard enough for it. All you have to do is work hard. My parents really believed this, and I believed it long enough to get me to college, where I learned to see this idea for the dangerous lie it is, one that doesn't take into account many things like, for instance, history.

The American Dream as taught to me by example, from two people brought to the United States from a Spanish-speaking country as children by parents fleeing a dictatorship and eventually given asylum as political refugees: In America, you might work like an animal, but you mostly get to keep what you work for. In America, the goal is a good job working for a boss you don't hate, maybe to be your own boss someday. This job has legit benefits, meaning health insurance and un retiro bueno that you never think about—the money siphoned off your paycheck each month and matched by your boss is just waiting for you, a pot of gold at the end of the workforce rainbow. The American Dream is buying a house in a safer neighborhood than the one in which you were raised, meaning your kids (the goal: two of them) will go to mildly better schools than the ones you went to, where you learned English the hard way and not through the invention of these ESL classes the more recent arrivals get—how unfair, you think, how un-American that these newer arrivals don't have to suffer the way you suffered. Everyone (except my future children) should suffer equally, meaning: as much as we did and no less—that is the American way! That suffering is what earns us the right to call ourselves Americans! It made us stronger, you will someday tell these two children of yours after relating horrific stories of how in first grade you were made to pee in your chair for not having the English words to ask the teacher—who shook her head at your begging in Spanish and said, "Maria, you must ask in English," her directive not even hinting at the noun you needed to say—to use the bathroom, the word *bathroom* a key you were to conjure from nothing.

When they are born, you give your kids white American names so that their teachers can't tell what they are before meeting them, so that your kids don't suffer the way you suffered in school, and so that they won't eventually be "inexplicably" denied apartments and jobs despite their abundant qualifications. You hope they can sidestep that pain, that confusion, and you are confident it will work as long as they play along when they need to, so you don't foresee these two children someday rebelling against these names and instead wishing you'd given them family names: Florinda, Hortencia, Milagros. One will eventually tell you she wished you'd named her Margarita.

If you happen to be male and straight, like my father, your American Dream involves earning enough money so that your wife (because you are married to a woman) doesn't have to work, and you can give her the gift of being a full-time parent. If you are a straight woman, your American Dream is to marry a man, move out of your parents' house, and then work as a nurse's aide or a teacher's aide for a little while before stopping that to have those two children. You therefore become part of someone else's American Dream—your husband's—where he earns enough so that he can give you the gift of being a full-time parent. Once those kids hit eighth grade, you can go back to work if you want, but only if the job has good benefits like un retiro bueno. Over the course of their lives, you take those kids on real vacations (meaning they last longer than the built-in breaks of a holiday weekend) where you drive to and from obscure American historical landmarks (a mountaintop in Tennessee, the site of the Civil War's Battle Above the Clouds). When things go well in this dream, you can take advantage of those holiday weekends and haul those kids to Disney World where, while waiting in too-long lines, you fantasize about being rich enough to someday buy the annual pass with no blackout dates. You fantasize about staying in Disney's Grand Floridian Resort for a whole five nights. You fantasize about being rich enough to buy anything you want just like that Trump guy on TV: a hotel, a golf course, a beauty pageant.

You fantasize about owning a boat. You go to boat shows. You fantasize about owning a Corvette. You go to car shows. One year's family vacation involves driving to the National Corvette Museum in Bowling Green, Kentucky, where you learn you cannot take the tour of the manufacturing plant because they are retooling the line for the new Corvette model. You get back in your van—the family road-trip-mobile you worked hard to pay for in cash—and you swear to yourself you will bring your family back here someday, only to forget about it for years and years (you've been busy working like an animal, remember?) until your wife, book in hand, maybe reads you these sentences.

■

My father's sister renames him whenever he comes up in casual conversation: She calls him Everett. She claims Everett is the English translation of Evaristo. If you ask various internet sources to translate Evaristo into English, it gives you: Evaristo. The red squiggly line of death marks it as wrong every time I type it in Microsoft Word, until I add it to the program's dictionary. Entomology says the closest English-language name to Evaristo is Evan, but even that is listed as a variant, not a direct translation the way, say, Juan is to John or Pedro to Peter. My aunt is wrong. In English, there is no Evaristo. In English, he doesn't exist.

The name Evaristo means "well-pleasing" and therefore does not suit my father at all. He was named after his god-father, a man who got hit by a bus on the way to my dad's christening, so the name was a last-minute switch. He was going to be called Reynaldo, after his father (my grandfather). Reynaldo instead became his middle name, and he undoes his parents' accident-induced homage by introducing himself as Rey whenever he meets someone new. But he goes by E.R. when he signs paperwork or anything even vaguely official, as if announcing himself an emergency. The initials have the added side effect of eliminating any suggestion of his ethnicity.

I've been told I would've been named Rey had I been born male. That name—with its sound (though not its spelling) meaning a line of light radiating from a bright object, or a very strange and mostly flat sea creature known to populate hilarious memes by photobombing (and therefore disrupting) people's Caribbean vacations—might've suited me better. And in Spanish, spelled the way they would've spelled it, it means king.

I have a sister, Kathleen, named after a nurse who'd been kind to my mother. That's pretty much the whole story. My mom had wanted to name my sister Jennifer or Amanda. Both names were extremely popular around the time my sister was born, a little over a year after I showed up. My mother tells this story of the woman next to her in her hospital room having had a girl, and when my mother asks what she's named her, the woman smiles and says, "Jennifer." My mother, four months into being twenty-two and already an overwhelmed mother of a newborn and a seventeen-month-old, supposedly turned to the kind nurse in the room and said, "What's *your* name?"

■

Jineane Ford aka Miss Arizona 1980 describes her girlhood self in a 2011 interview with *The Arizona Republic* this way: "I was not cool. I was not beautiful. My eyebrows grew together as a unibrow, and I had a big head of frizzy hair." (She and I had this in common.) In high school, she was a member of the science club (same), and she took classes to become a registered meat cutter (not so much). This certification included proving you knew the right way to skin what you were processing (the beginnings of a metaphor for a writing career, probably). I am certain my mother didn't know any of this.

■

When I was in elementary school, there was a girl—her name was Amanda Kindler—who was quiet and soft and wore a bow in her hair almost every day. She was on the jump rope team and had bangs that seemed impervious to Miami's humidity. I can't recall her voice, she was that quiet: She never talked in class and she whispered to her friends, of which I was not one. I was loud and joked around a lot, my best material straight rip-offs of the Muppets, mostly Fozzie Bear. (Gonzo's material only made me seem more awkward than I already was.) Every day, on our walk from school to wherever my mom had parked her car, my mom would gently encourage me to be more like Amanda Kindler by praising her qualities as feminine and desirable. She was such a good girl (which I heard, as it was meant, as her being good at *being* a girl in a way that I was not). She would sigh and remind me, "I almost named your sister Amanda." When I didn't get the message and instead kept working on my Muppet-inspired personality (while also insisting on wearing baggy T-shirts, tights, and a headband the width of an ace bandage to corral my unruly frizz—which, admittedly, made me look like I was perpetually recovering from a headwound), my mom's gentleness, in time, turned into direct provocation. "You should be more like Amanda Kindler," she began telling me outright on our walks to the car.

I couldn't understand why. While Amanda was very pretty in conventional white-girl ways (waist-length straight hair, ivory skin, the tiniest nose, gentle freckles), she otherwise did not seem particularly smart or witty or fun, or any of the qualities I valued in friends or in myself. She jumped rope like a robot: perfect, but she never smiled or broke a sweat, never seemed to be having any *fun* while doing it. She was, more than anything else, quiet. Very girly, my mother put it. Why can't you be more girly, like Amanda Kindler? I'd answer,

"So you want me to wear bows?" No, she would say, some-how dismayed at what I was: a too-skinny weirdo with buck teeth and a unibrow and way too much to say. I didn't like being outside, and I spent many afternoons crying and writ-ing, starting around second grade. I was sensitive in the ways that make many parents realize they have a budding artist on their hands. Those weren't my parents.

One day when I was in fourth grade, after picking me up and walking to the car together, after our automatic seat belts snapped us into our Toyota Camry's baked interior, my mother said, "I wish Amanda Kindler was my daughter." I can't remember what I said to that. I know I at least prob-ably thought, *Fine, go kidnap her, she won't even cry.* I was that kind of smartass. I also knew by then to keep my smart-ass comments to myself. My mouth was always getting me into trouble. But now I understand that she must have seen us both—Amanda and me, within seconds of each other— that afternoon as she waited with other parents to retrieve me from my classroom, and the contrast between what she thought a daughter should be and the daughter she had was too much to hold in any longer. This was not what she wanted, and she had to say it out loud to see how it felt to admit it to the only person who she thought could do something about it. She was maybe twenty-eight when this happened; at twenty-eight, I would still be coloring for fun and making pasta for every meal. By fourth grade, I'd already disappointed my mom by not being the graceful, elegant epitome of a beauty queen runner-up who she had expected me to be: I was, of course, my family's first manifestation of their American Dream, and she didn't like what their America was shaping up to look like.

Only now does it occur to me as strange and sad that my mother's ideal for a perfect American daughter was a white girl. Amanda Kindler did not speak Spanish, did not eat the same foods we ate, did not listen to the same music we listened to. Amanda Kindler needed to wear copious amounts of sunscreen to protect her from the sun we played under for hours without issue. Amanda Kindler was an American girl in ways I could never be, in ways my mother could also never be. Her ideal daughter was a white girl because she had long internalized the idea that as Latinx women, we'd be treated as lesser, that we *were* somehow lesser. And she just wanted better for me, which meant: whiter.

My sister named her daughter Paloma, and my mother celebrates the name, recently telling me, "Things are different now, you can be proud of being Latina, you can name your kids Spanish names." It's a position that strikes me as completely inaccurate from my place in Nebraska, where markedly Spanish names are still treated by most white folks with a sort of comic disrespect at best. (Ask my partner, Alejandro, how many times a Nebraskan has blurted out the chorus to that Lady Gaga song the second after he introduces himself.) At worst, the names are treated with outright disdain. (Ask him how many times someone has said they can't, or won't, say his name. Ask him how many times someone has suggested he use a nickname. Ask him how many times they suggested that nickname be Antonio Banderas.) But my mom's comment tells me a lot about the kind of America she thought she was bringing a daughter into. Be like Amanda Kindler: Be safe, hide yourself in plain sight; live up to the gift—the promise—of your white-girl name.

■

I am trying to remember when my mom stopped holding up Amanda Kindler as the epitome of girlhood to me—when she let go of her dream of a perfect American daughter and instead accepted the one she had. Amanda and I would go to the same middle school and the same high school, where a shift in our neighborhood's demographics meant she would come to be one of the few white students in our high school's population. She would end up a star on the volleyball team and the soccer team, physically stronger and taller than any son my parents could've produced. She would also come out as a queer woman. When this happened, I asked my mom if she still wished Amanda Kindler were her daughter. I meant it in a mean way, a way I now deeply regret, a way that positioned Amanda's queerness as something that should make her less desirable as a daughter. I didn't think of Amanda as less than human because of her queerness, but I knew my mother might. I knew her version of the American Dream included having a devoted daughter who would go on to marry a hardworking man—a man she could brag about and love as the son she never had. My mother's American Dream included being a grandparent someday. And although the latter was absolutely still possible if Amanda were her daughter, I wasn't going to be the one to point this out to my mother on Amanda's behalf. I wanted to rub my mother's nose in all of it, for having conflated what she wanted for herself—to be a white American girl who moved through the world with more ease—with what she'd wanted for me. The motivation behind my question was wrong, but the question itself would still elicit from my mother what I wanted her to feel: I wanted her to understand what a mistake it had been for her to hold in her heart a picture of the perfect American child that was not also a picture of me.

She didn't answer me. She hadn't brought up Amanda Kindler to me in years. Unlike me, she let go of it a long time ago.

■

According to her 2011 interview, Jineane Ford has her own business now. She restored Arizona's oldest lodge, and now she runs a restaurant and an antique store out of it. She struggled with her weight for years and eventually elected to have Lap-Band surgery and became a sort of spokesperson for the procedure. I don't know where Amanda Kindler lives or what she's doing, though I'm sure I could find her easily enough via social media. I'm not on Facebook, and I've avoided looking her up. As for me, I am a writer and a professor. I am still extremely fond of the Muppets, though I have long since accepted that I am more Gonzo than Fozzie. I go places and read from my books, and sometimes my parents are in the crowd and they look a little baffled. They seem surprised that the audience isn't solely comprised of people who know me personally—*who are all these people and why are they here?* While they understand that by many measures, I'm successful in ways they've learned to recognize, they don't totally understand how I did this while asserting—rather than muting—my ethnic heritage in my work. They don't understand why I would do this work when they'd given me what they thought was a key to escape it, a way of avoiding the work entirely.

At these events, people eventually ask me questions about things much more pressing than whether I've been to Cuba or why I have a misspelled white-girl name. I am sometimes asked by people who've read my fiction, what can we do to be better to immigrants? How optimistic are you about our ability to bridge divides between the new, Trump-fueled sense of tribalism emerging? I say to these mostly white crowds, this tribalism is not new, not for many Americans from marginalized backgrounds who've survived bigotry and hatred for so long. I point out that Donald Trump is a powerful manifestation of white supremacy; he and his administration's rhetoric and actions are not the start of such forces in this country, and my name is one small choice of perhaps millions made under their terrifying influence. I say, I am a novelist, a Latinx woman, a first-generation American. I am someone whose parents taught her that to survive and thrive in this country, I would have to work twice as hard as a white person. They never took issue with the unfairness of this; they said that's just how it is until the work itself leads to success that allows you to transcend the unfairness somehow. As a writer and an educator, I live in a similar nexus of reality and idealism, but I am not optimistic. If I stop paying close attention, academia can be a comfortable, recognizable place, one where I am encouraged to buy into the falsehood of a meritocracy that promises the American Dream to anyone willing to work hard. But I've come to see the American Dream for what it really is: a lie my parents had little choice but to buy into and sell to me, a lie that conflated working hard with passing for, becoming, and being white. I believed the lie for long enough to acquire the tools needed to dismantle it. I believed it for long enough to find the lock, to imagine my real self the key. I've turned it and the door is opening. The American Dream: a key you conjure from nothing.

I tell readers that I see it as my job to tell stories that encourage people to *act* on their empathy—not just to *feel* something, as feeling is not enough, but to be moved to *do* something substantial with those feelings, some action that works to fix the systems that required the need for books like mine in the first place. It's a vital job, one I love, and I know my answer is giving the person asking the question hope I don't feel. In 2017, at a library in Washington State, I said all this and other things, and then I stopped and rubbed my face. Then I said, look, a lot of times I feel this pressure to tell all you white folks that it's all gonna be okay and that you're all doing a great job. You're sitting here at this event, aren't you? You're good people. You want to be reassured. I'm not going to do that for you today. I can't and it's a lie. The real truth is that people of color didn't create these problems, and we don't have magical solutions to them that we are keeping from you. We're in more vulnerable positions than you are. We need you to solve these problems because it is costing us our lives. You are part of these systems yet refuse to believe how immensely you benefit from them. Losing privilege can feel a lot like inequality. If something feels unfair to you as a white person, it's likely that equality is actually being achieved in that moment. I told them about the gender imbalance in some of my classes, how there are usually many more men than women in the advanced workshops, how an exercise I created that ensured an equal distribution of time to speak felt, for those who identified as male, like it was skewed in favor of those who identified as women. I told this crowd, be aware of how you perceive things and how those perceptions are skewed, how you've been trained to skew them. I said all this and knew at the same time how little of it would sink in, how it is human nature to think of oneself as the exception, always.

I say something different to the Americans in the room who look and sound like me, or the ones whose histories mirror mine, the ones who come find me after readings, the ones

with parents as optimistic as mine were on the day they settled on my name. I tell those Americans, you and me, we have
ancestors who have survived much worse. Not just ancestors:
I'm talking about our grandmothers, our mothers, women
who've held us and seen us for the dreams we are, even as
they wanted so much more for and from us. We have privileges they never thought possible: We are standing inside that
privilege right here, talking about this. We have conjured the
key not from nothing, but from their sacrifices and from the
futures we glimpsed that sat just beyond the limits of their
dreams for us. We have yet to face anything as hard as what
they've faced and overcome. They've left behind—some by
choice and some by force and some through a combination of
both—more than we have yet to leave behind. That blood: It
runs through us. There is so much power in that, and so in us.

■

Ironically, in the end, my parents made the right choice:
Jineane Ford, 1980 Miss USA Runner-Up, ascended to the
throne later that year—through no work of her own—when
the original winner went on to win the Miss Universe competition. Pageant world rules apparently dictate that you can't
hold two titles at once, so Jineane got upgraded, and as sudden
as an accident, my parents had their beauty-queen namesake
promise fulfilled. In America, as the dream goes, anything
is possible. In 1996, a solid sixteen years after that night in
Carol City where my fate was sealed, the grandson of Ger-

man immigrants would come to own the Miss USA pageant. He would eventually sell it in 2015, just as he was ramping up his campaign to become the next president of the United States, a feat so many people were certain could never, ever happen. Not because he was the grandson of immigrants who maybe changed their family name so that it projected a power it did not yet wield. Not for the reasons that would stand in my way, or in the way of so many other newer or darker Americans. We keep learning, with every day bringing some new atrocity to light, that nothing is impossible in this America. Except perhaps eradicating the same long-standing bigoted forces, so well embodied by this country's current leadership, forces that prompted my parents, when searching for a good American name, to look to—and to hope for—not justice, which still seemed to them so far out of reach, but something more attainable and lasting: a kind of beauty.

MAGIC KINGDOMS

"Fantasy is part of the articulation of the possible . . . The
struggle to survive is not really separable from the cultural
life of fantasy, and the foreclosure of fantasy—through
censorship, degradation, or other means—is one strategy
for providing for the social death of persons."

—JUDITH BUTLER, *UNDOING GENDER*

N MY CHILDHOOD HOME, TWO PHOTOS ADORNED
the shelf above the TV for years—one of my sister, one of
me, each of us posed in front of Cinderella's Castle in Disney World's Magic Kingdom. My sister and I, ages two and
three, are wearing matching overalls with yellow T-shirts
underneath. I am smiling and have my head cocked, and my
long ponytail (made of thick, still light-colored hair that had

not yet been cut, a source of pride for my mother, her own hair dark and coarse) is pulled forward, draped over my shoulder in a way that clearly communicates the photo is a fiction: I've been posed by an adult, probably my mother, for this perfect shot. But my sister's picture is the good one. She will not be posed. She barely has enough hair for a ponytail; her hair sits in two poofs on her head like a set of homegrown Minnie Mouse ears. She looks dead on at the camera, clearly overheating (denim overalls!), refusing to smile, her eyebrows a straight line across her head saying, *Take your damn picture already and also I need a nap.*

This moment survives only because of the era: my dad's heavy camera on a belt-like strap, lens cap dangling from the lens, he cannot afford to waste film. This is all happening before digital photos and their infinite-seeming retakes, so my sister gets maybe two or three chances to make a face that perpetuates my parents' fantasy that she's having a good time, for all time. Considering how cranky she looks in the one my parents chose to frame and look at every day, I wonder just how awful the other shots must have been.

■

In the summer of 2017, I visited Disney World after a long hiatus. I'd last been there fifteen years earlier, as a college senior with my parents. College had given me an awareness of how popular culture operated and which cultures got buoyed by it, and which ones didn't. To put it succinctly: I made that

trip super not fun for my parents by pointing out every instance of the patriarchy's misogynist influence I could find.
I usually did this in the middle of a ride or a show, blurting
out my thoughts while we were trapped, the sweaty backs
of our thighs adhering to the plastic benches of whatever
boat, faux-log, or railroad car we were crammed into together.
I used words like *heteronormative* to describe any and all
things princess-related. I went back and forth on whether or
not the "It's a Small World" ride was unintentionally or intentionally bigoted; the former was forgivable and a place to work
from while the latter was not, I argued aloud to no one but
myself as the ride's never-ending song attempted to drown me
out. I wanted to show (and show off to) my parents how much
I'd learned, how much I now saw and couldn't unsee. They
spent much of the time wondering why they'd let me go to
college in the first place if all it made was a person who could
no longer enjoy things, who could no longer easily engage in
the version of fantasy Disney provides. They wondered aloud
what happened to their easily posed ponytailed daughter, the
one who could eat a Mickey-shaped ice cream without giving
them a lecture on *consuming and being consumed,* the kid
they'd taken to Disney dozens of times.

Then, a decade and a half later, I read an announcement
that the Great Movie Ride was being permanently closed down
in early August and—after a good five minutes of utterly baffling but completely instinctual panicked crying—I booked a
flight to Orlando with airline miles. My birthday, at the end

of July, was a handful of days away, and that was enough of an excuse to ride what had been my favorite ride (because the Muppet 3-D Movie does not count as a ride) at Disney's Hollywood Studios (which I still call MGM; my family went for the first time the year after the park opened, and that was its name then). Never mind that this is the kind of ride tired parents and old people always want to go on because the line is mostly indoors and air-conditioned. Never mind that it's recommended by bloggers dedicated to "hacking" the Disney experience (a vast corner of the internet you will most certainly drown in and which I do not recommend you look into at all) as good for riding during a rainstorm because the ride itself is super slow and something like twenty minutes long. Those were the best twenty minutes of nine-year-old Jennine's life!

I booked a cheap Airbnb right off the rundown strip of hotels featured in Sean Baker's 2017 film *The Florida Project,* a movie released in the United States a few months after this trip. My arms and legs and the sides of my stomach had begun to sear with newly sprouting poison ivy blisters. (Though I didn't yet know that's what they were. Having had no idea such an evil plant could exist in my Nebraska backyard, I spent a summer afternoon using my bare hands to pull up what I thought was just this weird ground cover.) The humidity and heat I was about to subject the rash to would make it so much worse, but I refused to allow any rational thoughts or actions to interrupt my enthusiasm. *I must go there*, was all I was thinking, *and ride this ride . . . One. Last. Time.*

I can now see that I loved the Great Movie Ride because it told several big stories very efficiently by dropping you in the middle of them. The slow-moving tram seating dozens of people at a time in long rows dragged you through recreated scenes from *Casablanca, Alien, Indiana Jones, The Wizard of Oz,* and more. The ride would pretend to stall out in one of the movies, and your trusty tour guide "driving" the tram would be replaced by some menacing movie character who'd hijack your vehicle and narrate a portion of the ride in a safely threatening way before justice was restored and your original tour guide saved the day near the ride's end, tricking the movie character somewhere in the Temple of Doom. I loved the whole thing because, yes, it was air-conditioned (which was extremely helpful on this trip, what with the July heat and the poison ivy blooming across my torso), but, much more important, it was the ultimate immersion in fantasy: I got to be simultaneously part of stories I loved and part of a new story happening in real time—a chaotic one that stemmed from the interrupted dream of the first one. The ride was, essentially, a metaphor for my existence as the American-born daughter of Cuban refugees.

■

The 2017 trip was my first and only time at Disney declaring a birthday. I don't know if it didn't exist or if my parents were just too shy to ask, but Disney has a ready stock of giant buttons for you to wear signaling the significance of your trip to everyone else. Your wedding anniversary, JUST MARRIED, JUST GRADUATED, FIRST VISIT, and the catch-all I'M CELEBRATING. If it's a life milestone, you'd best spend it with Mickey. When it's your birthday and you get one of those mega-buttons pinned on you, Disney employees working the restaurants sometimes give you free desserts. Sometimes they let you get in the FastPass line even if you don't have a FastPass. Sometimes they put you at the very front of a ride where having a first-row view makes a difference. Every single employee who sees you will say, "Happy Birthday!" and look like they really mean it. I didn't think about whatever training protocol demanded this response from them until I pinned my button to a corkboard back home.

The experience of celebrating something at Disney World is designed to make you feel like you matter, like strangers are sincerely happy you were born or happy you got married. Your own experience is forcefully and convincingly centered, while simultaneously, it's coarse-grained in a way that strips you (and your celebration) of its uniqueness. The entire experience is grounded in whiteness and heteronormative gender roles, essentially the world Disney has trafficked in for decades. During the days you spend in the parks, Disney will pretend you are white, American, cisgender, and straight, and everyone and everything around you will pander to and assert this understanding of the Disney fantasy. You see it in the food options, the ambient music, the manicured topiaries contorted to look like the characters Disney has worked for decades to ensure we've all grown up watching. Disney only purports to intentionally shift these norms in Epcot's World Showcase, where guests get to travel to countries like Mexico and Morocco without a passport, and where (some) parents can breathe easy knowing that a "safe" version of chicken nuggets—that quintessentially American kid pleaser of a meal—will always be on the menu, as opposed to, say, croquetas, or pastelitos, or any number of foods that, via their inclusion, would work to center something other than a purely American culinary experience. Still, it's powerful and validating to be so forcefully seen over and over again, even in this inaccurate, whitewashed way, and especially when it doesn't happen in real life, outside of the parks, where so much of our experience of American culture reminds us of how "other" we are in our America.

The fantasy Disney constructs, and in which it envelopes each guest, makes you genuinely happy, even though it's not a fantasy of your own design, but one intended to replace whatever you might've instead conjured for yourself; even though it's one that, in its execution, excludes and erases who you truly are. More important, by congratulating you on your birthday or your marriage or your anniversary at every turn, Disney's version of fantasy—one in which you are the center of their magic—makes you want to come back: to open yourself up again and again to everything Disney offers.

On that trip, I overheard an exchange among a white American family—a father and his two children, a girl and a boy, neither child older than ten—on the Pirates of the Caribbean ride (which used to be one of my favorites, up until that college trip when I actually paid real attention). I was sitting in the row behind them. The following is how I recorded their exchange in the Notes app on my phone.

DAD: They're closing this ride down soon to change it.
SON: Why?
DAD: Some women said it's offensive.
DAUGHTER: What's offensive about it?
DAD: You tell me.
[Watching as animatronic men hold chains attached
    to animatronic women, who are shackled by
    their wrists as they are sold off to other waiting
    animatronic men. Watching in silence now as the
    boat turns a little and animatronic women scream
    in terror as animatronic men chase them, the
    suggestion of rape clearly in the air. One or two of
    the animatronic running pairs have been switched
    since I was last there, so that the men are now being
    chased by the women.]
SON: I don't see anything wrong.
DAD: [Pauses dramatically.] Well there you go.
DAUGHTER: [Keeps watching. Keeps watching.]

I wondered at the weeks of work it would take in my class someday to undo this small moment in these kids' lives; the misogyny and violence inherent to it being normalized and so erased for them at such a young age, the way the father framed the offense being taken as something only women could feel. And I thought, if I say something—anything—it will totally ruin this ride for them, and I loved this ride when I was their age, the sense of adventure it inspired. I never thought to wonder why only the men got to have the adventure, or why, in a ride that pretends to be set in the Caribbean, the only language you heard was English. That Disney managed to convince a kid like me, with roots in the Caribbean, that this ride was more believable and real than whatever homeland my parents could conjure for me is a con job of the most magical sort. Disney simultaneously created and remedied (thanks to the ride's immersive fun) our own erasure. But why bring any of that up now from my spot behind them in our boat, when god only knows how much money this trip was costing this family, and I knew firsthand—because I'd been behind them in line—how long they'd waited to sit through this ride-turned-blockbuster-movie-franchise. The son was completely enraptured by what he saw. He was open and vulnerable in this rapture, and that's the exact moment when Disney fed him the same misogyny his father had just perpetuated.

Control the fantasy, and you control the people. The ride kept going and I said nothing.

■

When you say "park," I don't think, *space with lots of trees and grass where people play outside until they get too hot.* I think, word-association style, *Disney.* That I so deeply and intrinsically link Disney with the natural world might be a consequence of growing up in Hialeah, a city whose official slogan is "the City of Progress" and whose unofficial slogan is "Water, Mud, and Factories," though in South Florida, you're more likely to hear the slogan in its original language, where it rhymes: "Hialeah: Agua, fango y factorías." The tagline is in part a shout-out to the regular flooding that occurs in the city after it rains, especially in its industrial areas and around its canals. As reported in the *Miami New Times* in 2018, a survey company called WalletHub, which regularly ranks the hundred largest U.S. metropolitan areas in different categories, rated my hometown as one of the worst cities in America for recreation (ninety-eighth out of a hundred—Orlando took first place), largely because it has close to the lowest percentage of parkland of the cities ranked (ninety-seventh on that front). It's not that I have no memories of playing outside; it's that all those memories also involve scraped knees, bloodied from the concrete that seemed to be everywhere. The public park we sometimes went to (Amelia Earhart, which we visited mostly for birthday parties, as they charged a fee to get in on the weekends, and my parents worked during the week, when it was free) is bordered on the north by the Gratigny Parkway, so the swoosh of traffic always hovered close by. In the interest of providing complete information, Hialeah has also ranked as the worst city in other impressive categories, including financial security, living an active lifestyle, and celebrating Valentine's Day. According to WalletHub, there's a lot about Hialeah you might want a break from. (I can't help but disagree and think that someone at WalletHub has some kind of vendetta against Hialeah.) Regardless, when you've had enough of Hialeah's water, mud, and factories, a world of magic and ease (and free of cars, once a tram whisks you away from the parking lot) awaits just under four hours north on the Turnpike.

It wasn't until I saw *The Florida Project*, a movie about a girl and her mother struggling in every way possible to avoid homelessness, that a lot of my thoughts about the powerful role the parks played in shaping my experience of nature coalesced. In fact, it wasn't until the movie's final scene—which I won't completely spoil for those who haven't seen it—that I recognized this "shaping" as a manipulation. Disney has supplanted—and degraded—our own instinct for fantasy-as-survival with a ready-made version that fuses escapism with commercialism. The final moments of *The Florida Project* (which for the first hour or so I mistook for a documentary—if you've seen it, this tells you something about both me and the film) depict the escapist role Disney holds for many people so stunningly and so perfectly that the first time I watched the movie, my heart (but not my head) got the ending all wrong, feeling a surge of joy and hope for the two girls—the opposite of what anyone should've felt. The characters in that film cannot afford—in every sense of the word—the ending they're given.

For many Floridians, when it comes to getting away from it all, the Disney World parks are the equivalent of one-stop shopping. A big reason I didn't go camping until I was thirty-five is because, for Florida residents, park admission is drastically cheaper, so my family's idea of a weekend adventure was Adventureland at Disney. (Please note that "Disney" is what everyone I know from Miami calls all the parks and all of Orlando and whatever's around Orlando. As in, "I'm driving to Disney this weekend to go to my abuela's cousin's funeral.") Thanks to all that Park Hopping, Disney became—and sadly still is—my nature touchstone.

An example: At Smith Falls outside of Valentine, Nebraska, on a 2018 camping trip, I stood at the base of the state's tallest waterfall (which is actually a legit waterfall), inhaled deeply, and exclaimed, "Oh my god, it smells like Pirates of the Caribbean"—conjuring that particular scent of not-yet-mold that lingers inside the ride's fog. It's such a distinct smell that a Los Angeles–based fragrance company created a perfume to evoke it. The perfume's creator said in an interview with *Fodor's Travel* that, "Some people buy it to bring back childhood memories and others (like Disney fanatics) just love water rides and use the fragrance to feel like they're at a park all the time." He describes the fragrance as "chlorinated water, musty mildew (because the water doesn't get changed often), and the atmospheric damp fog in the air from the pyrotechnic/smoke effects." It's called Dark Ride.

Another time, trekking down the Niobrara River with friends, the sheer crust of the Sandhills towering above us, I craned my neck and yelled, "That part up there looks just like Thunder Mountain!" Another time, I spotted a family of turkeys, a mother and three babies. I realized I didn't know what a baby turkey was called—a chick? I tried a word out loud: *turklets*. This sounded very not right, and the silence in my mind following that ridiculous word was replaced quickly and reflexively by the song from Disney's Enchanted Tiki Room, which was often our first stop in the Magic Kingdom (our family being the kind that turned left after Mainstreet, U.S.A. rather than right into Tomorrowland). *In the tiki-tiki-tiki-tiki-tiki room*: On a loop, the memory of how the sound of the tiki birds' animatronic beaks clacking worked as a kind of percussion as they fake-sang. *A little louder!* the one bird serving as our master of ceremonies sings, and the volume goes up in my mind. Everywhere I turned, there was Disney World, showing me just how much it had asserted itself as my framework for the natural world—one that deliberately omitted any disasters over which I couldn't eventually triumph.

When it comes to the reality of Florida's most destructive natural disaster—the hurricane—the threat of one will sometimes actually *get* us to Disney: We bank on school being canceled, board up our windows, and drive north, annual passes in hand, dreaming of the line-less version of the parks we were sold when we bought those passes. The storm will turn at the last second and we'll be at the park celebrating by riding Splash Mountain five times in a row. It's the perfect plan if you buy into the fantasy that the storm won't hit. And even if the storm does make landfall, where better to be trapped than a Disney resort, which, in the days leading up to the hurricane, has a ton of cancelations from out-of-state travelers who had just rescheduled their trips in compliance with Disney's Hurricane Policy, which states you can rebook or cancel your room reservation with (mostly) no penalty if a hurricane warning is issued within seven days of your scheduled arrival date. All those empty rooms, some of them up to 40 percent off, and all you have to do is bet on what Disney's been teaching us since before we were born: that whatever catastrophic storm is headed our way, the story will have, at least for Floridians, a happy ending.

■

When I was in elementary school, we once came back from five days at Disney World—the longest we'd ever gone—and I was a wreck. In the days constituting reentry into non-Disney life, anything that evoked Disney caused me to weep. I have the distinct memory of raising my hand during a silent reading assignment and the teacher nodding me to her desk, and as I leaned in to whisper my question, I spotted a black-and-white photo of Mickey Mouse standing in front of the Epcot ball on her desk calendar. She'd outlined his ears and the ball in red pen maybe dozens of times. I fell silent and couldn't talk, just stood there crying and not breathing. When I couldn't stop, she sent me down to a counselor's office, where I cried harder (now that no one in my class could see me) and began to hiccup through my tears in a way that was disturbing enough that the counselor called my mother to come get me, telling her that I was sick. I don't remember anything after that—only the crying and the feeling that I'd been so happy at Disney World and I would never be that happy again. Disney had nurtured my impulse for fantasy—an instinct vital to survival but dangerous and ultimately damaging if misdirected. Our fantasies are not fantasies if they are given *to* us rather than imagined *by* us. We pretend our way into belonging when we feel we don't or can't belong because of forces outside of our control—our race and ethnicity, our gender identity, our sexuality—and the Disney parks are happy to assert (and insert, via the vast reach of their movies) themselves as a clean, complete, whitewashed system in which our imaginations can engage. And because of Disney's longstanding whiteness and the way that every cultural signifier in the parks works to affirm that whiteness, this means that built into its prescribed "magic kingdom" was my own erasure. Disney filled the openness it encouraged with its brand of false American optimism that pretends (and asserts) that nothing could possibly be wrong in this world as long as you believe in magic, a brand that perpetuated the very things my family was trying to escape by going there in the first place: a version of America where people like me grow up among water, mud, and factories.

∎

The impulse that makes Disney World the go-to escape for so many Floridians is the same one that has doomed the future of the state to the sea. The last time I went, I couldn't ignore what I'd already long internalized, in part because I'd loved the parks so much: the ways in which we'd been manipulated into ignoring and forgetting what was really happening around us both culturally and environmentally and calling such ignorance magic. Disney hides the trash, literally. The parks are run from underground, with maintenance workers and characters seemingly appearing out of nowhere. We don't see the work or the mess. It just doesn't exist, or it just disappears, and we pay good money for this bliss in the form of a three-, four-, or five-day pass. Of course we do, we go on vacation to get away from these things. And Disney helps us feel good about our choice to spend that vacation time in its parks, which have even begun to traffic in messages of conservation and environmentalism—a large thematic focus of Animal Kingdom's newest world, Pandora, and one if its newest rides, Avatar Flight of Passage (the ride has a specific focus on habitat restoration, which is hilarious when you think of the miles of swampland the area that is now Disney World once was). While watching Pixar's *WALL-E* for the first time (about a robot tasked with cleaning up Earth after giant corporations encouraged humans to trash it to such an extent that it becomes uninhabitable), I kept thinking, *How did this movie idea get past the pitch stage?* The movie is in many ways an indictment of all things Disney—all the humans in the movie are on an intergalactic cruise that's helped them completely forget about Earth's mess—and yet the day the DVD came out, I forked over my $24.99 so I could own a copy. Disney is so deep in me that I'd be first in line for a *WALL-E* ride.

It's not that I don't see the irony—I absolutely do (the DVD boasts "Earth (And Space) Friendly Eco-Packaging"). It's that Disney has somehow taught me that buying that DVD or standing in line for that as-yet-nonexistent *WALL-E* ride *does* somehow count as an acceptable and worthwhile response to climate change. Or that buying the *Moana* DVD, which of course I did, and then watching it multiple times with my niece and dozens of times on my own, somehow undoes the misogyny and racism embedded in the fantasy the parks perpetuate.

■

The first time my parents ever went to the parks was on their honeymoon. My aunt and uncle spent their honeymoon in Disney World, too. So did my partner's parents, who live not in Hialeah but in Westchester, the same neighborhood Richard Blanco so lovingly details in his memoir, *The Prince of Los Cocuyos: A Miami Childhood.* Blanco has a whole chapter devoted to his first visit to Disney World, a pivotal moment for any child, but especially for Latinx children who've never left South Florida—in part because of the gringo gauntlet you have to traverse to get there. Blanco describes how "Miles away from Miami, everything felt so exotic, so American" by cataloging the change in landscape and language, a dislocation that primes his childhood self for the wonders and relative safety of the Magic Kingdom. Blanco doesn't mention them—because I suspect they went up after he was already grown—but ask any Miami kid about the billboards for Yeehaw Junction and they will tell you how many miles they signified you still had left to drive. Blanco does, however, describe an encounter a couple of hours into the trip between a gas station clerk wearing a Confederate flag belt buckle (a flag Blanco has never seen and can't name as such) and Blanco's father: The former is hostile toward the latter's Spanish-accented English. This scene takes place when Blanco is eleven, in 1979, but it's replayed itself thousands of times with different kids and different parents, mine included. Whenever our parents drove us all to Orlando in search of magic, they never explained why they refused to give in to our childish pleas to stop at something with a name as ridiculous as Yeehaw Junction.

You didn't have to go as far as Orlando to encounter Blanco's exotic, fantastical America. In high school, some friends and I left the familiar palm-lined streets of Hialeah for the foreign city of Davie, about twenty-five miles north of us, in an attempt to go country line dancing. We dressed for the occasion: any shoe that looked like a boot, anything with fringe. The whole adventure felt a little like heading out to a cowboy-themed Disney park. I wore a choker with feathers hanging from it, deciding it was sufficiently "country." But once we piled out of the car and saw the people in line, we did the opposite of Blanco's attempts to try on Americanness: We acted even more Cuban. We became the loud spics everyone thought we would be, speaking in big Spanish even though we normally spoke to each other in English. The guy guarding the door spit into the dirt as we flashed him our learner's permits, lowering his cowboy hat *exactly* the way one lowers one's cowboy hat. Other people in line snickered and shoved as if being directed from somewhere off camera. That night, we became, like Florida itself, a peninsula of warring factions that, in the end, came just short of colliding on a Davie dance floor. We never got in; the doorman turned us away for reasons we didn't understand. (It was a sixteen-and-over night, and we were all old enough.) Like Blanco, even just twenty-five miles north of home, I felt like we had entered another country. A cowboy spits; a carload of Cubans heads back to the country they came from.

And growing up in that country—the imagined country of Miami in which I could pretend that every American was also Cuban—provided me with an experience similar to the fantasy world imposed by Disney, with one crucial difference: With Miami, the fantasy was of my own making, and therefore part of "the articulation of the possible," Judith Butler's claim that articulating our own self-designed/imagined fantasies helps us create, for ourselves, a place to exist and survive and even thrive in the face of a reality that dictates otherwise. No wonder we wanted to head back to our Miami the instant this foray into Davie contradicted the fantasy that had given us the confidence to head north in the first place.

Visiting Disney is, for many Miami-raised Latinx kids like us, our first time leaving one fantasy world for another. Our first time around so many white Americans, it's an experience that has the potential to erase and replace our fantasy for an unattainable homeland, planted in us by our parents, with an idealized white-centered version of paradise. It worked that way for Blanco. There's a tender moment in his memoir when, as he enters the Magic Kingdom and sees Mainstreet, U.S.A. for the first time, he is so overwhelmed by its beauty and perfection that he turns to his mother and asks if this is what Cuba looked like. His mother responds with what any Cuban reading this knows is coming: Of course not, Cuba was even better. You have to wonder, though, if all those fantasies our parents and grandparents fed us about Cuba—especially about its idyllic, natural beauty—didn't set the stage for a place like Disney World to swoop into our imaginations and become the kind of promised land we could actually visit (for a price). We could even take a boat ride through it, see and smell it, chase the phantom of that scent all our lives until we find it in an aptly named perfume. Thanks to the fantasy of Cuba our families built in our minds, a Cuba we could never know even if we grew up to someday visit it, we were well practiced in longing for places where, as the song promises, anything your heart desires will come to you.

Honeymooning in Disney meant that my parents' future visits would be caked in an extra-sweet layer of nostalgia. I can imagine them there, just barely out of their teens, newlyweds in line for Space Mountain. They'd never been on anything like a roller coaster before; imagine the adrenaline of that big unknown coming on the heels of another—their first night as married people, their first time together without a chaperone. Like many Cuban kids coming of age in the United States in the 1970s, they'd been vigilantly chaperoned for years by the time they married—they got engaged when my mom was fifteen—and the thrill and relief of finally being alone together after such a long and formal courtship really is the stuff of fairy tales, Disney or no Disney. Of course they wanted to take their children there as soon as those kids were potty-trained.

■

I have a new favorite ride, now that the Great Movie Ride is gone. It's the aforementioned Avatar Flights of Passage, which I rode for the first time during that rash-addled trip, and which profoundly moved me—figuratively, not literally, as it's a 3-D virtual reality-type ride that only makes you feel like you're flying when in fact you're just clamped down by the waist next to several other people. The brace that comes

up behind you and squashes you into a center console initially irritated me, this time literally, as it pressed into the
band of poison ivy, which, by that stage of the trip, circled
my torso like a belt. The premise of the ride is that you will,
via an avatar, be riding the banshees we saw in the film *Avatar*; we're being given this opportunity as part of the Pandora
Conservation Initiative (the video leading up to the ride tells
us that we're a part of some important conservation/popula-
tion rebuilding research). The point is you go into the ride
feeling great, so you keep waiting for the twist—the moment
when everything goes wrong in the lab, or when your banshee
loses its mind and tries to throw you off or something, a classic formula for many of Disney's more formidable rides. But
none of this happens. Over the course of this incredibly immersive sensory experience, you're provided with a vision of
conservation efforts that double as entertainment. Also, you
will swear you are fucking flying.

The result is almost transformative. The ride was like
a recurring dream of flight I'd had and would have again,
even that night, except that in this latest dream, there was
now a magical creature doing the flying work beneath me.
The fantasy Disney gave me overrode what had long been a
version where I was doing the flying, a version I'd had since
childhood. When the ride ended—a moment that is intentionally and disturbingly abrupt—I yelled, "No!" as if something
precious were being ripped from my hands. Two other people
in my group did exactly the same thing. As of this writing,

there is nothing like it. Without a FastPass, the wait for this ride was more than three hours long. People suffer through it and afterward say it was worth it. They sometimes get right back in line.

While strapped in, I forgot about my poison ivy entirely, but it was there waiting for me when the ride was over, searing in the places where the mechanism that had held me in my seat had just been, making it so much worse. And all the while, I hadn't even noticed. By the time the fantasy was over and the adrenaline wore off and the tears cleared (yes, I cried at the ride's end, much like I did at my teacher's desk in third grade, when I first felt how Disney had both given me something while also taking something else away), the welts and blisters were so angry, there was nothing I could do but hope and wait for the pain to subside. It all took far too long to heal.

■

My niece is following in her mother's childhood footsteps. Every picture we've been sent of her while at the parks has her squinting in disgust at whatever my sister has gleefully presented to her. Disney now has a service where they take the pictures for you, perfectly staged at designated spots around the park, and my sister sprang for it for my niece's first visit. As of this writing, the service costs two hundred dollars, but you can save thirty by purchasing it in advance.

The pictures are magically delivered to her phone and viewable in the My Disney Experience mobile app.

My sister dragged my niece back to one particular photo spot, in front of Cinderella's Castle, three days in a row to get the perfect shot. My niece kept inadvertently ruining the fantasy this service promises to provide with her facial expressions, which repeatedly lead you to believe she's either melting or actively shitting her diaper. One of the best photos catches her nestled next to her grinning parents and rolling her eyes. Her apparent distaste for the parks so far might stem from her sense of being overstimulated; she's two, so everything is already a fantasy. She's not ready for Disney World to override her already impressive imagination with its branded version of generic white American happiness. She doesn't need to be told how to be happy. For now, she's happiest back in the air-conditioned hotel room, with her diaper on her head as she dances to songs only she hears.

For 2019, my sister and her husband bought annual passes, the platinum ones with no blackout dates. My niece doesn't need one: Like all children under three, she gets in for free.

II

VARIOUS

IMMERSIONS

SAY I DO

ONCE UPON A TIME, IN PROPER FAIRY-TALE FASHION, a man asked me to marry him. This invitation was an excellent life development. It meant, among other things, that a wedding would happen, and I would get to plan it. I love planning, both in theory and in practice, and I hadn't been given the chance to organize an event with this many moving parts since co-chairing my high school's prom committee (though I take no credit for the vapid theme, "A Walk in the Clouds," as that was voted on by the seniors). I would deploy all my event-planning skills, and my wedding would turn out even more amazing than prom had because this time I was totally in charge. I was twenty-three.

Our wedding budget was limited enough that we'd opted to forgo a DJ and instead create a wedding playlist we'd blast through a rented PA system. This choice ended up being the proverbial straw that broke the camel's back for my mom, who had already started to worry that our various money-saving choices (choosing a Sunday date, for instance, or having my uncle officiate an outdoor ceremony at the reception site instead of holding it in a church, or only having three bridesmaids instead of nine or ten) were undermining the seriousness of the event. We were doing weird things that would make guests uncomfortable, she argued, like handing out programs. She'd never been handed a program at a wedding! Why give out pamphlets explaining who everyone in the wedding party was when everyone should already know, because of course every bridesmaid is some guest's adult daughter. When she said *guests*, she meant my side of the family: the Cuban and/ or Miami-based guests. Cubans don't have three bridesmaids, she claimed, they have as many bridesmaids as they have female cousins and second cousins, even if they barely know these women. Cubans didn't do programs, only Americans did that. Did I think I was a gringa all of a sudden?

Maybe I did, now that I was marrying a gringo—the

groom was a white man (we'd met in college), and I thought
that meant we needed programs because an Emily Post wedding etiquette book, gifted to me soon after my engagement
by an older well-meaning white woman, said so. She'd given
me this book after indulging my riffs on ideas for the party
(and it was, for me, above all else, a party—one where I just
happened to be making a lifelong commitment to someone
near the beginning). She was concerned, after hearing my
money-saving idea of eliminating salad from the buffet (which
no Cuban I was related to would eat anyway) that there were
things I just wouldn't know about how white American weddings were done, and she thought Emily Post would help.
Which is why I found myself making wedding programs by
hand, printing out the various pieces of them at work a little at a time, when no one was looking. My mother watched
me thread ribbon through cardstock to bind pages together,
shaking her head and wondering why I was wasting my time.

But not hiring a DJ, that's where she drew the line. A
reception without a DJ wasn't a reception at all, she argued.
Then she convinced me she was right by offering to cover the
expense of one herself.

This development wasn't exactly the best news for the
groom. He'd looked forward to building a playlist with many
of his favorite songs, which admittedly weren't the jams I'd
grown up hearing at receptions. (He has what many people
would consider excellent taste in music and refuses to pander
to popularity or nostalgia, two qualities that I'd come to learn

characterize the go-to songs of most wedding DJs.) I don't remember if we discussed what Spanish-language music would be on the playlist, but it went without saying that any substantial salsa, merengue, bachata, and/or reggaeton selections on the list would be there because I'd put them there.

Of course music is important at a wedding reception. But in the discussions with my fiancé about this particular aspect of the planning—we had very different tastes in music, to put it lightly—it was clear something weightier was emerging: He and his white monolingual American family had a very different idea of what a wedding reception looked like, the kind of music that would be played, the whole atmosphere. In wanting to control the playlist by doing the music ourselves, he was working against the idea of a cheesy American wedding DJ, a type I hadn't encountered enough to even register as a type. (I'd been to only two white American weddings in my life by that point, and my concept of this DJ type was largely conflated with my memory of Adam Sandler's character in *The Wedding Singer*, and so I imagined these theoretical DJs sporting slight mullets and too-skinny ties, their mouths pressed against microphones that amplified slick, faux-deep voices.) Yet in my experience as a Miami wedding goer, the typical wedding DJ either was currently or had previously moonlighted at Power 96 (aka "Miami's Party Station" circa 2005) and/or had a residency at a South Beach club (assuming you weren't already holding your reception at said club, in which case you'd want your DJ to have a residency at a *differ-*

ent club). Ideally, your wedding DJ's name would be Laz, and his equipment would include several barely legal pyrotechnical devices. He would be too cool to talk to, and—aside from announcing the names of the wedding party—he would not need to talk during your reception very much at all, because he understood his turntable skills would do the talking for him. Basically, I'm describing the DJs at the weddings of my various high school friends and cousins, who were all pricier versions of the DJs from their proms. These were not receptions my soon-to-be husband had yet experienced.

In the seventeen months I'd given myself to plan the event, I began to worry that elements of a wedding reception that seemed totally standard to me and my family would be viewed as some kind of spectacle by certain guests. I'd never been to a South Florida wedding reception for a Cuban couple that didn't have a cigar roller, for instance. A dude in a guayabera sitting at a table behind a stack of tobacco leaves was as typical at a wedding reception as that long line of female cousins all made to wear the same unflattering dress (another decidedly American wedding thing: allowing your bridesmaids to pick their own dresses). But having lived outside of Miami and gone to college and graduate school in predominantly white places, I knew how quickly elements of the reception could turn into edutainment for the white guests, how whatever we put in front of them could become a story that would represent all Cubans to them for the rest of time, because the wedding weekend would likely be their only experience being among us. I imagined them heading back to small-town Illinois or Nebraska, ordering a "Cuban" sandwich at an upscale midwestern bakery, and using that as an opportunity to launch into a completely unrelated story about my reception. I hoped the DJ we hired could help me at least complicate this probably inevitable moment by serving as the bridge between the two cultures, musically. If he played some solid white-people tunes, the white folks would have no choice but to feel included. (I want to acknowledge that I never imagined the DJ as a woman, which speaks to how I've been conditioned to think of the person in control of the whole event identifying as male, that only a man could do this job. If I were to do it all over again, that's one of many things I'd change.)

When I told my fiancé we had the money to hire a DJ—and that if we were going to keep my mom happy, we didn't really have a choice but to do so—we agreed that we needed one who would understand this cultural divide and figure out a way to bridge it. We needed a DJ who could, as the reception unfolded, anticipate and address both the possible discomfort of our white American guests based on their perception of being excluded; and also the tendency of the white American guests toward exotification: that the reception would be not an event to experience and enjoy, but to view from the outside as spectacle and, usually, with some judgment. In college, I'd seen my life and my approach to living it turned into white people's teachable moments over and over again, and on my wedding day, I wanted none of that. I thought the way around it was to show them my awareness of and an appreciation for *their* norms. The complication here, I thought, was that this wedding was happening in Miami, where the wedding DJs seemed indistinguishable from radio and club DJs. Meaning, they weren't exactly feeling out a crowd for its cultural norms and catering to them so much as they were setting those norms for the club-going set. I felt like what I was hoping for was impossible, and I worried—because I am a writer—that my concerns about this aspect of the wedding planning were really just a metaphor for something I wasn't yet ready to admit.

Was I overthinking this? My mother thought so. But this approach of pleasing everyone some of the time had already informed another major decision, which was to conduct the ceremony in both English and Spanish, the same words said in alternating paragraphs, my uncle serving as our bilingual officiant. This choice meant a longer ceremony (which is not something Emily Post recommends), and it meant that for about half the time the groom's entire family—himself included—wouldn't understand what was being said. Most of the younger members of my family speak both English and Spanish, but the older generation—namely my grandparents and their siblings and cousins, who would all be there—only spoke Spanish. Though they'd be left out of the English portion, they hear enough English every day not to feel discomfort around it—that had been their reality since arriving in the United States. This was not the case for the Americans visiting from central Illinois or the suburbs of Omaha: Spanish was not, and had never been, a regular part of their lives. But it was also not the case for the white folks coming from California, who, like many whites who live there, had managed to construct personal and professional lives where—despite being in a state with a large percentage of Latinx people, many of whom speak Spanish on a daily basis—they seldom had meaningful interactions with anyone nonwhite. By having a bilingual ceremony, everyone in the room would understand at least half of what was being said. It was the most inclusive option, and so that made it the best one.

The groom and I agreed I would interview DJs in Miami while he continued preparing for his Ph.D. preliminary exams in Illinois. The first guy was recommended to my mom by her hairdresser; she'd already met this DJ at the salon and, as was clear to me from her repeated claims of his hotness, had developed an instant crush on him. (To be fair, he was pretty hot.) She invited him to her job over our lunch hour—I was working the front desk there that summer—so that I could meet him, but she was already sure he was perfect. He went by DJ Freddy J, he was Cuban, he shaved his arms, he had a slick-backed thicket of black hair with an admittedly excellent fade, he spoke both Spanish and English, and so, in short, my mom thought this was a done deal despite having no idea what he was like as a DJ.

At both of the white American receptions I'd been to prior

to my own wedding, at some juncture the DJ played a couple of country songs in a weird, nostalgia-laced way. This never happened at Cuban weddings—at least not at the ones I'd been to. While I didn't want the DJ I hired to bust out Garth Brooks (the only country artist I could name at the time), I did want to know what he *would* do, what he knew about white American weddings and what he could bring from that knowledge into this one, seeing as many of the guests (most of my college friends included) were white.

I planned on asking DJ Freddy J of Hialeah Gardens if he knew, for instance, of the chicken dance. I knew nothing, but I had heard about this poultry-themed display as a thing some white people liked to do at their weddings (Emily Post must've missed this, but I'd heard about it from some of my groom's relatives). I didn't need Freddy to play whatever the chicken dance was, but had he at least *heard* of it? Say one of the groom's uncles, three sangrias into the party, asks him to play it: Could Freddy show me how he'd politely and respectfully decline the request?

I began the interview by asking Freddy the following paragraph of a question (which I'd written down beforehand, proof of the extent of my worry): "So, Freddy, many of the guests will be Americans not from Miami. My future husband is a white dude from California whose parents were raised in the Midwest, and some of his family is flying in from places like Illinois and Nebraska. As you already know thanks to my mom, we are super Cuban. All I want is for the reception to be an amazing party. What will you do to be sure everyone has a great time on the dance floor?"

Freddy wasted no time. He tugged on the cross hanging from the gold chain around his neck and answered in Spanish, which he was more comfortable using, but I will provide the answer in English, though it loses much in translation: "Look, okay, the first thing you gotta do is," here he placed his hands on the arms of his chair, lifted his body out of the seat, pulled his right knee into his chest, then kicked a flexed flat foot high into the air between us while making the impact sound from *Mortal Kombat*, "kick all those Americans out of there. They don't dance. They don't *nothing*. They are dry and they're just gonna sit the whole time anyway, so that's step one, forget about them. That's a lost cause."

At this point, the interview should've been over, but my mom was giggling like a girl in love, wiping at her eyes and saying, "That's true, I tried to tell her!"

Many white people I've met often think of themselves as culture-less, as vanilla: plain, boring, American white. What they are revealing when they say this, which they often do in jest, is how little race impacts their lives, how whiteness is ubiquitous to them, and they mistake that ubiquitousness as a kind of neutrality or regularness that renders their race and culture invisible to themselves. But from the outside, we see their culture in a way they don't—or maybe couldn't, at least not until after the 2016 election, when the majority of white people who voted did so for Donald Trump, who essentially ran on a version of whiteness. That election compelled some white people to look at themselves, at their whiteness, and to wonder what being white—something they'd never really thought about at all—might mean. Good for them, seriously, but it's an evaluation that DJ Freddy J of Hialeah Gardens had, in 2006, already concluded about white people as reception guests.

Freddy went on to tell us that what I wanted was impossible and therefore I should cater only to the Latinx guests, who were the only ones who knew how to party. Freddy also, it should be noted, kept referring to himself in the third person as DJ Freddy J.

I told Freddy that his response was not an acceptable answer. He said, with more authority than I'd ever said anything at that point in my life, "Well, my bad, but it's true."

He laughed big and so did my mom. I knew then I wouldn't hire him. But it turns out the hiring wasn't up to me, and Freddy figured that out faster than I had.

He proceeded to flirt with my mom in a way I recognized, because it was the way I knew Miami guys to flirt: leaning forward, shoulders and traps flexed, head held at a slant as he winked and scrawled his sentences in the air with his hands. He encouraged her to bond with him over how ridiculous he found our chosen wedding song, "It's Only Time" by The Magnetic Fields. He hadn't heard of the song or the band and dismissed both with a wave of his hand as "white people shit," and my mom sighed in relief and agreed; she hadn't heard of them either. They also bonded over berating me for thinking I could "get away with" putting Daddy Yankee's tired and mildly misogynist reggaeton hit "Gasolina" on my no-play list. Freddy took issue with the fact that my fiancé and I had created a no-play list at all—he claimed he'd never heard of the concept and felt it would hinder his craft, because no song should be even theoretically off limits to a real DJ. He waved his hands at the paper and said he didn't need to see it. When I insisted he look over the list, he smiled at my mom and asked her what my deal was. She rolled her eyes and shrugged and said, "See what I'm dealing with," as if she'd already warned Freddy about me.

Strange things were happening in that room, and one of them was that I was starting to see myself on the white side of things. I wanted a DJ who would help center a white experience—the particular white American experience of a Midwestern-in-origin American who Freddy could not imagine because he'd never encountered it. Because in Miami, the white experience is also typically a Cuban one: To be Cuban in Miami was to be a kind of white, with all the privileges and sense of cultural neutrality whiteness affords. Of the three people in that room, I was the only one who knew this, because I was the only one who'd left Miami for long enough to see what being Latinx meant from the outside. I was the only one who had known the feeling of being a nonwhite adult. (I specify adulthood here because it bears mentioning that my mother's first years in the United States, in the late 1960s and early 1970s, having left Cuba in the Revolution's wake, were a crash course in how nonwhite she was; Freddy, though, had come from Cuba fairly recently, as a teenager, to a Miami already colonized by people with the same last names and language as the people he'd left behind.)

I wasn't able to articulate any of this thinking then, but even if I had, I wouldn't have felt the need to do so, because I was not letting this dude anywhere near my wedding. He'd insulted half of my soon-to-be family, mocked me in ways that made me feel like I was in middle school again, and saturated the room with his Drakkar Noir cologne—also a 1990s Miami middle school throwback. I think the only question my mom asked him was if he would be so kind as to take out his earrings for the event—his earrings being the only thing about him I wasn't opposed to—and he told her, for her, *anything*.

Once he left and I began the chore of airing out the office (lest the smell trigger a second puberty), I was very clear with my mom: No way were we hiring DJ Freddy J. No way were we taking any more recommendations for DJs from her friends. I'd find some names online and set up times to meet them once I was back from that weekend's bachelorette events in New York City, where my sister was living.

She waited until I was out of town to hire him. She mitigated my anger about this by telling me she'd talked to him and made my expectations clear. My fiancé was rightfully upset, as was I, but there comes a time in the planning of any wedding where you stop giving a shit and just hope for the best. Also, she was paying for it. I did start to worry that I had made a bigger deal out of it than I needed to, that maybe the way the reception unfolded would not turn into a metaphor for larger cultural divides in my relationship that felt insurmountable. Maybe it would all be fine if I just ignored it— more proof that the brand of whiteness my almost-husband practiced was taking solid root in me.

Two months later, Freddy played "Gasolina"—the top song on my no-play list—not once but twice during the reception, prefacing it the first time by announcing to the crowd that it was my favorite song. As predicted, when he played merengue or salsa songs, certain guests would stand and move to the dance floor, and when the music shifted to something more contemporary and in English, those guests would sit and my college friends would head out. I remember only one song where almost every Cuban sat down and every American got up to dance: a weird mash-up medley of songs from the late 1950s and 1960s that included "Rock Around the Clock." The spectating switched up for that one, with my relatives watching as white folks paired off and busted out dance moves heretofore unseen by their eyes. When the music turned to dance hits from the 1970s, that's where Freddy succeeded best: Everyone seemed to know what to do. He could've answered my thorny interview question with that: The answer is always disco. Perhaps nothing brings people together on

a dance floor, regardless of ethnicity, more than the voice of
Gloria Gaynor singing "I Will Survive"—a hit I would've been
happy to hear twice.

■

In the intervening decade, I've gained much more experience
with white people's weddings. Were I to marry a white man
now, I would have a much better idea of how to construct an
experience in which all the white folks present could feel comfortable partaking. For instance, say you want your wedding
to be classy yet understated: The answer is you hold it in a
tastefully restored barn, and not a parrot-infested jungle island theme park in Miami Beach, which is where I held mine.
(And which is why, within minutes of saying "I do," my groom
and I were handed a skunk for a photo op, the skunk being
the "other additional animal available" that was contractu-
ally promised to us by the venue, along with some parrots,
for said photos. Please note that skunks and parrots are not
traditional elements of a Cuban wedding reception.) I owe the
bulk of this new white wedding knowledge, ironically, to my
divorce.

A handful of months after my marriage ended, I moved
across the country to Lincoln, Nebraska, with the narrative of
"starting over" in my head. Just as the narrative of a wedding
usually includes one (or two) white dresses, the divorce narrative typically requires the renting of a fantastic downtown
apartment that has nothing in common with the suburban

home my former husband and I had just put on the market. The one I found was gorgeous (twenty-foot ceilings!) and quirky (it used to be a major government building—you can live in what used to be the city mailroom!) and seemingly perfect for the young hip professional single person I would undoubtedly become once I moved in. I felt this way about my new place pretty much up until the first weekend I lived there. That's when the weddings started.

That first summer alone, I attended more than a dozen white people wedding receptions without ever leaving the comfort of my bathroom. The building I'd chosen to live in liked to think of itself as Lincoln's premier wedding venue. I was not told this when I signed the lease, but a glitch of duct work sent the sounds of every single event in the building's reception hall straight through the exhaust fan of my apartment's bathroom, so loud and so clear that I could hear the names of everyone in the wedding party as they were announced—not just in the bathroom, but from the living room. I could hear when people were clapping, each clap an individual sonic event—I could almost always make out the crisp echo of the last person clapping. I heard every word and every song every DJ played, and my former husband had been right to classify them as straight-up cheese.

The building manager also neglected to mention that the apartment next to mine was at that time not an apartment at all, but was rented out as the bridal suite, and so I often ran into the brides on my way back from the gym (going to the gym a lot is also part of the divorce narrative) or while grabbing my mail. I always wanted to say something to them, something wise and funny but mostly anything other than *congratulations*; I was, after all, still someone fairly fresh off a failed attempt at what they were now trying out, and I wasn't so much bitter as I was sort of protective of these women. I didn't want to stop them from getting married. I just wanted to ask them if they were sure—*really sure*—that they knew what they were doing, that this wasn't some automatic decision they made because they'd been with someone a pre-scribed amount of time, or they had hit (or recently passed) the age their parents were when *they* got married, or they were scared to be alone, or any of the dozen or so reasons I kept cycling through as being why I'd gotten married years earlier, none of them feeling exactly right. Every time I encountered a bride this way—almost always slamming into her and her en-tourage as I was coming or going somewhere—I said nothing, and the lack of an automatic compliment or a congratulations from me was usually registered on her face as an omission I hoped would turn into some sign, if she was looking for one.

The building's receptions became a crash course in the white American weddings Emily Post's book had been talking about, the ones I'd been looking to borrow from. (In the two years I lived there, I witnessed zero receptions where the cou-ple wasn't white and heterosexual. That said, I eventually got so sick of the weddings and their DJs invading my apartment that I sometimes went out of town on the weekends—perhaps

the brown/black/queer wedding receptions happened then?)
I started keeping track of patterns I heard from my bathtub.
What follows here are my carefully observed and extremely
scientific findings, should the twenty-three-year-old version
of me out there need them.

About two-thirds of the time with these weddings, there is
a moment deep into the reception when the DJ stops the party
to say that the groom would like to dedicate a special song
to his bride, and that song is almost always Sir Mix-A-Lot's
"Baby Got Back."

You must have a bridesmaid named Ashley or Katie.

The white people version of "Gasolina" seems to be either
Garth Brooks's "Friends in Low Places" or Billy Ray Cyrus's
"Achy Breaky Heart" or Rednex's "Cotton Eye Joe," depend-
ing on how well-off the family seems.

The following interaction occurred several times my first
summer living there: A bridesmaid and her boyfriend or a
groomsman and his girlfriend stumble down my hall, thinking my doorway is a safe place to sit and have The Conversation She Needs to Have with Him *Right Now*. In all my
time living in the building, this only happened with straight
white couples, which speaks to the power of the privilege
they have—that they can have arguments about their most
intimate relationship problems in random hallways without
fearing harassment or stigmatization. Typically, one of the
people involved in this bold dispute is named Taylor or Tyler.
In each of these instances, Taylor/Tyler wants to know *where*

this is going. The male partner is very confused as to why they have to talk about this *right now* when they were not even five minutes ago having a great time on the dance floor at their big sister's/brother's wedding reception. The stakes feel very high for the suddenly weeping female partner because she's just witnessed an event that makes her judge her own life as lacking: She wants the dress, the flowers, the cake. The woman in these exchanges, every time I've seen her, has been in tears, careful eye makeup obliterated, face patchy with red. Both have been drinking; their words are slurred, their postures sloppy, the points and evidence they each try to bring up poorly argued. I know this because I could hear their entire conversation word for word from my bedroom as clear and as loud as if they were in bed with me.

The cake at these receptions is pretty basic. I know because I started going to the receptions and eating the cake. I considered it fair compensation for hearing "Baby Got Back" and/or "Cotton Eye Joe" twice a weekend. And it was the least these families could offer me after having to politely and repeatedly ask Taylor/Tyler to please, please, *please* take their conversation elsewhere so I could go to sleep. I didn't want to cost the couples and their families any more money than they were likely already spending, which is why I only went for the cake. I knew firsthand that each place setting at dinner had a price tag.

From my bedroom, I could clearly hear the DJ announce when it was cake time, and after hearing everyone either laugh (because the bride and groom had shoved cake in each other's faces) or say, "Awwww" (at choosing not to do that), I would throw on a black dress and head down the hall.

The very first time I did this, it hit me hard that I wasn't in Miami anymore—most if not all of the guests were white. There was no way I could pretend to be related to anyone in the bridal party. From that moment, I knew I couldn't pass as a relative like I could back home. Here I'd have to be some-one's friend from work, or maybe someone's nanny, or maybe part of the catering staff. Over that summer, I tried them all out with varying degrees of success. I watched people the way my former husband's family had watched mine: with cu-riosity and judgment. All these white people were dancing to anything and everything the DJ played, and then it hit me: Their DJ was one of them, and they were all on their own turf. I never danced, knowing whatever I did with my body on a dance floor would make me stand out among the white folks (I'd already learned this years earlier at college parties). I never tried to drink, never approached the bar. And I made sure to stay far away from the gift table.

Sometimes, along with a slice of cake, I took a centerpiece. Sometimes I did this near the end of the reception, but some-times I waited until after, when I'd just pull them right out of the building's garbage. Many Cubans claim centerpieces early in the reception by dragging them right in front of their plate at the table the minute they sit down. I once went to a wedding where the mother of the bride had the DJ announce to us guests to please leave the centerpieces in the middle of the table until after dinner so they'd look good in the photos. It's a known tendency, is what I'm saying. Nebraskans apparently had no such tradition, which I found shocking and even wasteful. So that summer I almost always had fresh flowers in every room of my apartment, a fact that usually offset the depressing nature of the manner in which they'd been obtained in the first place.

I did not keep this activity a secret. In fact, I told people about my wedding crashing, though I didn't call it that for fear of evoking Vince Vaughn. When asked, I would say that I did it to prove a point: If your reception is invading my apartment, then I'm going to invade your reception. But in hindsight, I think I was going to these receptions to punish myself. I'd been the one to initiate my divorce, and I had no clear, tangible reason for doing so except that, when I was honest with myself, I could admit that what Jennine in her twenties needed most from marriage was emotional stability and future security (qualities that had even tinged my search for a DJ, the person I wanted to be responsible for making everything go smoothly), and then, as I got older, that need fell away. And I knew we each deserved more than I was giving. In the video of my wedding—which we watched for the first time on a whim years after, on some anniversary—minutes after saying "I do" and just after cradling a skunk in our arms, the person filming asks me how I feel. "The same," I say, looking straight at the camera. "I feel the same. Marriage is just a piece of paper." As we sat on the couch and those words hung in the air, "the same" seemed like a very fucked-up answer. I couldn't look at myself on the screen or at my then husband. We never watched the video together again. We discovered, in that one and only viewing, that I'd accidentally taped over almost the entire ceremony weeks earlier. The footage overriding the ceremony was of me whisper-laughing as I recorded a white man doing what he'd called "authentic karate" on stage at a physics department talent show. I got to keep the tape in the divorce—more punishment, I think. I never thought I could be the kind of person who would accidentally record over their wedding video—irresponsible, careless—but I also never thought, long before anyone ever proposed, that I would be someone who was divorced.

Despite my new ambivalent feelings toward marriage and its limits, I understood that *weddings* weren't marriages; a wedding has little bearing on a marriage, in the end, except as perhaps a metaphor for the seeds of its discontents. I now see that my wedding was, for me, a self-designed rite of passage into adulthood (and perhaps into the privileges of whiteness) that I desperately needed, one my family could understand and definitively accept, one that would have the side effect of making my choice to pursue a writing career acceptable to them because a highly educated man from a good American family had agreed to be legally attached to me for all time.

I saw a version of this desire in the receptions I was crashing; all first marriages (from what I could tell), a sense of having just crossed the threshold into adulthood suffused every party. In grabbing a slice of cake off a table, eating it calmly while standing near some great-aunt as she discreetly tried to place this short, dark-haired, definitely-too-brown-to-be-a-relative guest standing before her, I assuaged any feelings of guilt at crashing by thinking of myself as contributing to the uniqueness of the bride and groom's event, as helping to sweep them into this new phase of life. I was part of the Unique Package, "unique" being the quality I'd learned every Nebraskan couple aims for, at least to some extent.

I learned this fact, too, in the building's reception space, when it played host to an annual wedding fair. I'd never been to one while planning my own wedding, perhaps this was where all the ideas were handed out? It was open to the public and on a Sunday. I went, slightly hungover, in my pajama pants.

"We make sure every wedding is unique," one vendor told me while gesturing to a mason jar with a candle in it. I'd wandered over because she was giving out chocolate samples.

When asked, I told most of these well-meaning vendors I was a bride-to-be or the sister of a bride-to-be (and thus a very invested maid of honor). The one thing I learned quickly *not* to say was that I was divorced, as this got me politely shunned from whatever free sample they were offering up to the blushing first-timers. "You only get married once!" they kept telling me whenever the subject of something's cost came up. Being too honest about myself meant acknowledging that people were spending a hell of a lot of money on something that ultimately had no guarantee, no matter what promises we make to ourselves and others. Outing myself as divorced threatened their whole shtick, the very thinking—*you only get married once!*—that's helped make weddings a seventy-two-billion-dollar-a-year industry.

"The mason jar thing is so over," another vendor told me. Mouth full of bacon-wrapped dates, I asked what, then, is the new thing.

"Industrial Modern or Bohemian Classic." I nodded like I knew what this meant and she added, "We're seeing a lot of unique things come out of those themes."

Weddings need themes, I'd just learned. No wonder DJ Freddy J had had such a hard time: I hadn't given him an appropriate theme to work with! And I should've been aiming for "unique" rather than searching out the kinds of things that would've made my wedding *more* like the ones our white American guests had likely already been to. Based on what I was hearing from my apartment every weekend—the DJs' playlists barely varying from reception to reception—one of the most unique things a Lincoln-based bride could *really* do was hire and fly in DJ Freddy J. This choice alone would make it the most unique white wedding ever.

Once I had enough free food in me and been plied with enough brochures and price lists to paper the walls of my apartment, I confronted one of the DJs—the cheesiest looking one, who'd set up all his lights and was talking into a microphone even though it wasn't on. He was why I was really there, wasn't he? He was the one my former husband had envisioned playing at our wedding, the one I couldn't imagine. Now I couldn't get away from him. He was the one filling my bachelorette pad with a cacophony of reminders that lots of people were in love and happy, reminding me that I was no longer someone's bride, reminding me that I'd known from the very beginning that I was worrying about the wrong things. He was the one making me feel as if I'd devolved into a sad little rat scurrying around the fringes of a wedding reception, picking at leftover cake and flowers in an effort to figure out why I couldn't be happy inside of something that I'd been taught was designed for my happiness.

I did not say hello or introduce myself. I spoke to him with the kind of barely contained rage that, in Miami, you reserve for the person ahead of you in line at a bakery when you overhear them order the last pastelito de coco.

"Do you do a lot of weddings in this building?" I said.

"Oh yeah, yeah, I do most of them, actually." He winked at me and it was such a forced, ugly thing that I didn't even think of DJ Freddy J when he wooed my mom into giving him the job. "I'm in high demand," he said.

"That's great," I said. "Do you realize that everyone on the west side of this building can hear every word you say inside their apartments?" I didn't know if this was actually true—in fact, I'm now fairly certain it was just my apartment—but I didn't want to sound alone in this.

"Whoa, that's weird!" he laughed.

Elton John's "Crocodile Rock" came on over his speakers. The DJ had a mustache and a mullet and was wearing a gold vest. My former husband's worst DJ nightmare, right in front of me for the first time. My hands went numb. Like watching the coconut pastelito go into the box.

"You say the same thing at every wedding," I said. "You play the same songs in the same order."

This was a fact. I'd started listing the songs in a notebook once I'd suspected it was happening. This laziness offended me so much that I wanted to tell the brides afterward even though it absolutely didn't matter.

He said, "Yeah, well . . ." and then dropped his eyes to his laptop as if there'd suddenly been some iTunes emergency.

There is nothing like having a middle-aged wedding DJ ignore you to the tune of "Crocodile Rock" to make you realize how different your life is from what you thought it would be. He began ignoring me as if knowing before I could that I'd never need to hire a wedding DJ ever again. I thought about DJ Freddy J's foot in the air with a mimicked *doosh*, kicking out all the white people. I had a track record with men in this profession sending me subtle cues about how my life might unfold. Through the speakers, Elton John joined in with the wedding fair DJ's oblivious mockery of my life choices: *Naaaaaaaaah, nah nah nah nah naaaaaaaah.*

I didn't know what I was doing there, not just *there* as in trying to pick a fight with a wedding DJ, but there as in divorced, in a job I hadn't seen myself taking, in a geographical state my high school best friend and I jokingly banished each other to when we wanted the other one to disappear. I didn't know what I was doing there, and the strangest part is that it felt okay that I didn't know—or more accurately, the sensation of not knowing felt right, which hadn't been the case for a long while. In fact, I'd been avoiding that sensation ever since saying yes to someone when they offered to spend their life with me. I could've never imagined myself in any of the roles I now inhabited, and yet now I was these things. I'd told the DJ what I'd observed, and what had come from all those careful observations? Say he told me to get out of his face, say he blushed and hoped no one had heard what I'd said, say I slammed his laptop shut and got myself kicked out of the wedding fair. Say whatever you want, because ultimately, the DJ just wants people to dance. I was the only one saying anything, trying to get at what I had wanted to be part of, and then, having lived it, no longer wanted: That's what I've been trying to say.

Behind me, another DJ—not a vendor but one hired by the wedding fair—announced that a bridal gown runway show was starting. His voice was my excuse. He asked everyone in the hall to have a seat in some chairs arranged around the runway, so the women modeling the gowns would have at least a handful of people in the crowd. Let's say a couple dozen of us listened. Say I wandered over, sat there in my pajama pants, registering that every bride was white, was wearing white—and that in looking around at the white faces that had joined me, I understood I was the only person there having these thoughts. Say I accepted this, and that I said nothing, because I knew where I was.

Say I knew, at least, where I didn't belong.

GOING COWBOY

ONE OF THE FIRST THINGS I DID WHEN I MOVED from Florida to Nebraska was find myself some cows to herd. It seemed like a must when considering one of the state's claims to fame: There are over three times as many cows as there are people within its borders. I'd moved to the state to take a job at the University of Nebraska in Lincoln, the state's capital and its second largest city, and learned before my time there officially began that roughly 25 percent of the incoming class would be first-generation college students. I had this in common with them, but there was a key difference: Many of these first-gen students came from rural backgrounds, from families where work centered on cattle and corn. I'd grown up in Miami, had gone to a high school whose population rivaled that of some entire Nebraskan towns. With the last few weeks of summer ahead of me, I decided that to be better at my job, I needed to see the real Nebraska, whatever that meant.

I eventually found a website for a ranch in a town that some folks considered to be the rodeo capital of Nebraska. (*There's a rodeo capital?* I thought.) Aside from what seemed to be easy access to cattle, the ranch offered visitors a chance to stay for days or even weeks at a time and work from dawn until dusk, to experience what it's like to be, as their website put it, a *real Sandhill cowboy.* The website also promised that this was a real working cattle ranch; no spa day, no golf or yoga, it warned. I would be *driving the herd*, it said. "The Sandhills proves to guests there is a lot more to Nebraska than flat lands and cornfields!" I read in that exclamation point my defense of my own hometown: *There's more to Miami than South Beach!* I should expect to spend at least six hours a day on a horse; I would get my own horse for the duration of my time there. I'd never been on a horse for much longer than it took to take a picture of me on one.

Upon calling to confirm the trip, the woman on the phone—

who turned out to be the wife of the rancher, the whole enterprise of getting tourists to pay to work the ranch being mostly her idea—told me to be sure to bring a hat. "A cowboy hat with a stampede string would be best," she said. I wrote down *stampede string* to google later and asked if a baseball cap would suffice. "The tops of your ears will burn," she said. "But if that's what you have, that's what you have." I told her I didn't sunburn easily because—and here I stuttered, covering up what I almost said with the phrase *because I'd grown up in Miami.* I'd been living in Nebraska for about two weeks, and it hit me at that moment in our conversation that with this new home state came very different demographics and assumptions: Leading with the fact that I was Latinx (which in Miami is all but assumed) might make my hosts a little less excited to meet me. Just as I'd never spent time on a ranch around white folks, this woman had, more than likely, never meaningfully interacted with a "Latino Hispanic"—as Republican candidate Donald Trump would mistakenly come to call us during one of the presidential debates. This was the summer of 2015, and this call took place just days before Trump announced his run at the Republican nomination by slandering all Mexicans as rapists and murderers. It wasn't until I caught myself trying to avoid mentioning my background and masking my Miami accent that I realized my ranch host might be afraid or suspicious of someone like me, feelings that the next year would only amplify—a year that taught me to be very afraid of my new white neighbors.

The woman laughed into the phone and said, "Well! I don't think we've ever had someone from Miami come stay with us." Her big, easy laughter scooted us right past any other questions about me. She gave me the heads-up that there would be a film crew there for part of my stay. "Some French folks," she said.

The French folks turned out to be four guys who never bothered to clarify their names to me. They were boy-bandish in nature; I thought of them as "The Leader," "The Wannabe Leader" (he was the main character in the documentary), "The One with the Long Hair" (their camera person), and "The Other One" (destined to be forgotten, his presence is blurry in every picture I took). They arrived at the ranch a few hours after I did and, strangely, by cab: They'd flagged one down at Omaha Airport and somehow convinced the cabbie to drive his minivan more than two hundred miles to drop them off. Before the cabbie drove away—another two-hundred-mile return drive ahead of him—I ran up to his window, through the cloud of cigarette smoke the French guys had created within seconds of getting out of the cab, and asked him the fare. "Over five hundred bucks," he said. "Those jerks didn't even tip."

They were at the ranch to film part of a documentary about completing an American-themed Bucket List for French Hipsters. They were doing everything American; they'd come to this ranch to be *real American cowboys*, they kept saying. And they wanted it all on tape. They'd flown into Omaha from Chicago, where they'd just completed another French-designated quintessential American Experience: going to a Cubs game and eating a deep-dish pizza.

They wanted to play cowboy but they came to Nebraska? I asked nobody. Prior to this trip, I hadn't known there was a significant cowboy and rodeo culture in Nebraska. The Nebraska I imagined was just flat fields of corn—and that's true for most of the parts you can see from I-80—but I didn't know that much of the state rolled with cattle-covered hills. The cowboy boots I'd sometimes seen on the feet of people in Lincoln were not, as I'd originally thought, some kind of quirky or subversive fashion statement; these people were legit. The mud wedged under the heels should've given that away, but I had my own assumptions about Nebraska, and none of them included cowboys. My own imagination placed all cowboys in one of two places: Texas or Wyoming. It hadn't sunk in for me yet that Wyoming, a state I'd grown up thinking was the definition of the middle of nowhere, was now right next door.

I'd shown up to the ranch wearing a pair of extremely clean and not-at-all-broken-in black leather boots, a pair I'd bought in Davie, Florida, years earlier when my dad, after becoming an American citizen, dragged our family north of Miami for an afternoon to buy everyone real American cowboy boots. I'd owned the pair since I was fourteen and had worn them maybe twice; I wore them to the ranch thinking they would help me blend in right away—a kind of disguise, along with the plaid shirts I'd bought at a Lincoln thrift store for a quarter apiece the day before. The rancher noticed the boots immediately as I approached his barn and asked me why I was wearing ropers. Days later, I learned that ropers are a style of boot with a shorter heel than standard boots, typically worn not for long distance rides like the ones we'd be doing, but during rodeos, when a cowboy would need to slip in and out of a saddle's stirrups more quickly than a standard boot heel allows. I looked down, lifted a foot off the ground as if the correct answer to his question were written on the bottom of my boot, and answered him by saying, "I think these are just boots?"

His mustache hid whatever his mouth did before he turned away.

I learned the next morning that I'd been assigned a horse named Katie, which I took as a good sign. I'd loathed a girl in college (for good reason!) by the same name, and here was the universe, giving me a chance to make amends. Both Katies were plain, dull-yellow blondes, nothing distinguishing them as memorable in appearance. The rancher assigned Katie to me in part because he (correctly) sensed that I was afraid of horses and she was their nicest, most mellow horse (the same cannot be said of College Katie). I was to brush her, feed her, get the saddle on and off her each day. The horse looked at me like she'd seen enough of my kind and was not looking forward to doing most of the heavy lifting in our relationship.

The French guys argued with the rancher over their horse assignment, wanting animals that would play into a certain narrative in their film and not the calm, admittedly unremarkable horses with which we'd all been matched. I can imagine these guys planning out this part of the film while still in Paris, smoking cigarettes and sitting around their third bottle of wine, dreaming of their version of the American West, each of them atop a sleek wild beast looking exactly like the marbled jumpy horses the rancher didn't dare trust us around, the ones still in the pen. I almost sympathized with them. The Wannabe Leader felt he'd been given a smallish horse on purpose and asked the rancher to reconsider, claiming the horse would make him look silly and weak and "not like a tough man." I suspect the rancher knew this and that was *exactly* why he'd assigned him that horse. When the rancher ignored him, he traded horses with the Leader, whose horse at least had some freaky blue eyes (the negotiation of this trade happening in whispered French). The rancher responded only by intentionally confusing the names of these two men the rest of the time they were there.

A thirteen-year-old girl who volunteered on the ranch was tasked with showing me how to put on (and later remove) Katie's saddle by myself. When she saw how nervous I was just to come up close enough to the horse's side to do this, she tried to assuage my distress by telling me she'd been riding horses since before she learned how to walk. I was impressed, but this revelation didn't make me feel any better. Not at all. It made me feel my foreignness more, despite, I think, her hope to do the opposite. This offered-up fact of her life seemed unimaginable to me—as unimaginable as the claims made by Nebraska students and new neighbors I'd later meet that they'd never seen the ocean in real life. I'd grown up going to the beach, a place some of them—when faced with the concept of the sheer vastness of the ocean—described as terrifying. As terrifying, probably, as the moment I first slid my foot into that saddle's stirrup.

After several days of herding, I had a strong sense that the rancher wasn't a huge fan of the French guys. (For good reason, as they often rode their horses very quickly in directions that he didn't want them to take, filming the unauthorized galloping and spooked cattle along the way, which meant more hours of work for him.) I wasn't much of a fan either, in part because they were showing me the ugly side of what I was really doing there: They were there to say they'd been there, to have it mean something about the kind of people they thought they were. They were there for the story of it—and I was doing the same thing, really, hiding behind the excuse that it would make me a more empathetic professor. Like them, I was using the relative foreignness and perceived exoticness of the rancher's day-to-day life as a form of entertainment, or perhaps edutainment, since I entered into it hoping to learn something I could take back with me and apply to my interactions with other Nebraskans. My curiosity about his world was not in and of itself a bad thing, but when the rancher joked over after-work ice tea and vodka that in this country, "Things certainly have changed. I met my wife in Gun Club,"

I snuck away and typed the exact phrase into my phone. I'd been doing that since I'd first arrived, my curiosity converting into a kind of touristy voyeurism as I documented things he or his wife said that revealed just how much distance there was between my version of America and theirs. Even if I'd convinced myself I was coming from a place of sincere inquiry, I still harbored expectations, and the setting in which we'd found ourselves allowed for the kinds of quick stereotypical judgments I was all too willing to catalog every time the rancher fulfilled them. He had pointed to my car from across a field minutes after I'd gotten there and asked me, with a sincerity I can only describe as Nebraskan, "What kind of car is that? A Prius? Who makes that car?" I was suddenly aware of how teal my car was. I'd answered, "Toyota?" He made no other response except to stare a few seconds longer and then walk away. From that distance, I could see my car as he saw it: a giant misplaced Easter egg from somewhere overseas.

Did the rancher see himself differently, either in that moment or later, because of the way *I* looked at *him*, with surprise and confusion for not knowing which company manufactures the Prius, a car that—in the various American cities I'd lived in—was as unremarkable as Katie the Horse? Perhaps he hadn't experienced the same flash of self-awareness as I had, maybe because he likely saw me as another tourist, not so different from the French guys—someone with enough free time and extra money (things I learned ranchers rarely have) to actually pay to work on his ranch. I can admit that if I were him, I'd have trouble taking people like me seriously. I could think my wife was a genius for coming up with a scheme like this while also quietly resenting her for the extra work these visitors sometimes made for me. No one had yet asked me what I did for a living, so no one knew I was about to be a professor at the big school a few hours southeast. If asked, I didn't know if I would even answer with that fact. While true, it didn't feel totally accurate, in part because I've always thought of myself as an accidental professor, someone who came into the job because of a whole other career as a writer. I suspect the rancher didn't actually care what we did in real life; it had no bearing on his own, what time he had to be up or how many hours it would take to track down the herd's bull—who was (and is) always alone—to make sure he looked healthy. When I joked that he should just track the bull via GPS, he didn't grin *or* frown, and the neutral mouth behind his heavy mustache was worse than either because by then he'd assessed what I still hoped to prove wrong: that we would never, ever understand what the other's life was really like, and worse, he'd decided long ago that there was little point in making the effort.

■

One morning, I snuck cookies from the previous night's dinner into my saddlebag for that day's ride: The six hours a day on a horse turned out to be a conservative estimate and I needed snacks. Cookies were a bad choice, though, because the chocolate in them melted in the heat and left my hands sticky, and also because the rancher took to calling me Cookie Monster once he caught me eating one while on my horse, yelling out, "Let's go, Cookie Monster," every time I'd lagged too far behind or got my horse in the wrong spot while trying to pen cows.

To shake off the Cookie Monster label, I tried to be on the rancher's side when it came to dealing with the French film crew. Over dinner one night, the Wannabe Leader tried to talk to us all about wine (there was no wine on the table; the rancher was strictly a spirits man, from what I could tell). I knew enough about wine to understand what he was talking about, but I kept that knowledge tucked away that night, instead turning to the rancher with a face that said, *Can you believe these fancy jerks?* The Frenchman then began talking about how us Americans ate turkey on the Fourth of July. "Why do you do this?" he asked, and even though I realized right away he was confused—he meant Thanksgiving—I kept my mouth shut.

One reason why the Frenchman was talking as much as he was might have been the fact that during every meal, from the minute we walked in, the TV perched at the end of the dining table was on and permanently set to Fox News. The volume on low, no one really acknowledged that it was on, but it seemed to me that everyone at the table was watching and not watching, the hum of hatred unacknowledged even though we could all hear it. The Frenchman was trying to drown it out, which was more than what I was doing. After hearing the rancher go off about Mexicans getting free passes into the United States—he used the word Mexican as a synonym for Hispanic, and I was, I learned in that moment, passing as white to him—I was too afraid to ask if we could perhaps change the channel.

The rancher's misinformed grievance about Latinx Americans is one I hear often because, as a light-skinned Latinx woman, I often accidentally trespass into moments that are essentially displays of white power intended only for other whites. It wasn't until my first year of college, when I read Nella Larsen's novel *Passing* in a course, that I first recognized this trespassing as an act in which I had sometimes found myself but didn't yet know how to define: White people who misread me as also white sometimes display the kind of pervasive racism usually reserved for white-only spaces. They inadvertently include me in these white power moments, ones that we aren't supposed to witness, which are perpetrated by the kind of well-meaning white folks—people who genuinely don't consider themselves racists—when they're sure we aren't around to hear them. I once walked out of a spin class at a Lincoln gym because, in the darkness of the room, the trainer (almost correctly) assumed everyone in the room was white, and she'd begun the class by shouting her excitement that we were now *on the road to making America great again*. This was the day after the 2016 election.

Larsen's *Passing* also taught me, at age eighteen and living outside of Miami for the first time in my life, that passing for white was something one could do *on purpose*. Years later, I'd find myself in Lincoln doing just that while looking at apartments, but only after having flat-ironed my curly hair and wearing my glasses instead of contact lenses, to hide, I guess, behind the frames. I'd told myself I was just trying to look professional, but I knew a euphemism when I heard it. Here is the ugly truth: I didn't want to miss out on a good apartment because of someone's ignorance, and that meant doing what I could to look whiter. On a walk-through of the place I eventually rented, the young white woman showing me around complained out of nowhere that the previous tenant's food was *really smelly*, saying, "He was Indian, so . . . you know." I said only, "Indian food is delicious," which meant: Please continue to think I'm white and therefore as complicit in your racism, because I really want this apartment. It was a stance I could take in part because of my light skin and the privileges it affords, and I felt guilty for intentionally accessing such privileges. Now, this same light skin was keeping me safe at the rancher's table—a protection I'd accessed unintentionally but that I was afraid to voluntarily give up once he'd made it clear how much he hated people like me. But in not giving up that protection, I was helping him perpetuate his ignorance by choosing instead to ensure my own safety.

Which is another word for comfort. Meaning, something I could afford to relinquish, something we must in fact relinquish, if we have any hope of changing each other's minds.

I did not have the privilege of knowing which of those two words—safety or comfort—would prove more accurate.

■

The irony in the rancher's anger about Mexican immigrants getting free passes for citizenship—an anger that is based on falsity spread through the propaganda he consumed along with every meal—is that there is a Latinx group that, at the time, did benefit from that kind of special treatment. That privilege, which could be described as a free pass to citizenship, had been extended (for many years and for many complex reasons) to Cubans. Meaning, to my parents. The rancher had no idea that the manifestation of one of his greatest fears—the American-born child of these immigrants who were taking everything, everything—was sitting at his dinner table. That she'd been hired, in fact, by the public university whose football team he followed as closely as his religion. Look at me, taking their jobs. From his perspective, by just sitting there, I was proving his point. And yes, I may have literally paid him for that seat, but didn't my soon-to-be salary come from his own tax dollars? Lord, if he only knew what was right there in front of him. He had no clue how right and how wrong he was.

I now look back on the trip and can't believe I went up there alone in the first place. If I hadn't been raised in Miami and thus tacitly taught to consider myself as a kind of white, I would've known to question my safety sooner. "I don't think we've ever had anyone from Miami come stay with us," the rancher's wife told me when I'd called, and it wasn't until I was driving back to Lincoln that I thought: If I were any darker, I would've learned a long time ago that the safest move is to avoid the kind of people I just left behind.

There is no way I would make this trip now. I'm too scared to head into the rural parts of Nebraska, where I'm not sure I count as American despite being born here. More than that, in the time since the election, I've lost the desire to know what life is like for a certain type of Nebraskan, a certain kind of American. And that's the scariest part of this story, learned in the aftermath of the trip: I'm as ready to make judgments about them as they did about people like me when they voted for the Republican candidate. The night of the election, after the race was called, a group of ten or so young white men wearing American flags as capes marched down the street in front of my apartment building, a main drag in Lincoln, cheering and chanting "Lock her up!" It was almost two in the morning. Their yelling woke me up. In my half-sleep, I heard the phrase a new way: The "her" they meant was me. I thought of the rancher, how his complaints about Mexicans were really about policies that applied only to Cubans, how I left that fact unacknowledged out of fear—I thought about how these boys could be his sons, and I felt grateful that I'd kept my mouth shut, that I'd left the ranch without any confrontation. The phrase I thought was, *I left in time.* I wondered how much longer my light skin would keep me hidden from them.

■

The rancher had only one thumb, the result of having swung a bad dale with a lasso. "The speed and heat from the rope take it clean off," another ranch guest—this one a regular from Colorado who came back season after season for a work-vacation—explained to me. "You see a lot of old rodeo guys without thumbs," he said.

I never acknowledged the rancher's missing thumb, or that the word "dale" (pronounced DAH-lee) is taken from the Spanish word the Mexican cowboys—vaqueros—yelled as they tossed their lassos. It's a skill American cowboys took from them. I looked all this up once I was back in Lincoln because hearing this Nebraskan saying "Dale!" as if singing along to Pitbull's latest made me think there had to be a connection between the words. I wanted there to be one; I wanted desperately to link these things—to show how history and language could work together to lead this Sandhill cowboy to yell a stolen Spanish word every day of his life without even knowing he was doing so. I wanted to find the right detail, make the right discovery that would open up his heart and make our lives seem less foreign to one another. Or, if that seems more and more impossible with each passing day—as he chose to keep Fox News on at the dinner table, signaling to anyone there what kind of America he believes in—at least it could open up someone else's heart, perhaps yours.

I don't know if the rancher knows the origin of this word, of how it ended up in his mouth. The connection might seem to him as strange as finding a French film crew playing cowboy on his ranch. Or as upsetting as realizing that a few days in a saddle will actually teach you very little about the lives of many of the people you are about to encounter. Or it might be as jarring as something I felt on my last day there: sitting on a horse, my eyes closed, the Nebraska wind rolling over the Sandhills and thrashing miles and miles of waist-high grasses and sounding exactly like the relentless wash of waves against a Miami shore. There was no denying it. There was no drowning it out.

THE COUNTRY WE
NOW CALL HOME

I.

OVER THE PAST SEVERAL ELECTION CYCLES, whenever discussion turns to Florida, talking heads can't help but drift to the topic of the Cuban American vote in Miami. I used to be part of this vote, but my out-of-state move has me playing a new role in every election: that of an unofficial Get-Out-the-Vote advocate to a dozen or so very disillusioned Cuban voters, the two of most immediate concern being my parents.

Months before Donald Trump secured the Republican Party's presidential nomination, signs dotted lawns all over Miami-Dade County proclaiming "This is Rubio Country." These signs might as well have just said, "A Cuban American family lives here." Even if they weren't exactly fans of Rubio, for many Miami Cubans the prospect raised in the Republican primary of having an American president of Cuban descent was too inspiring not to embrace. (Ted Cruz, of course, didn't count.) Let Puerto Ricans have the first Latinx Supreme Court Justice; us Cubans would go down in history as being the first Latinx Americans to make it all the way to the White House.

Because they rarely leave Miami, people like my parents took the literal signs in support of Rubio as a figurative one that he would win the Republican primary. As early primary states started coming in for Trump, my parents kept saying, *How is this happening? Who are these people voting for this clown?* Trump's robocalls saying, quite literally, "Don't vote for a Cuban," were working. Then it was Florida's turn.

The electoral map of the Florida primary results showed the peninsula as a solid Trump red, punctuated by a big blue dot at its end—Miami-Dade County, self-proclaimed Rubio Country. (The image of that spot of blue at the bottom of the state prompted a slew of jokes on social media about Rubio getting "just the tip.") Gone was one version of a historical run at the presidency—one many Cubans were hoping to see.

For years I'd bemoaned the fact that my parents were largely one-issue voters: the issue being a candidate's stance on Cuba and the embargo, since anything directly or indirectly supporting the Castro government was out of the question. But I embraced this tendency once Trump locked down the nomination, urging them to please vote for one reason and one reason only: to prevent a Trump presidency. This urging, though, began before we knew for sure who I'd have to beg them to vote for.

Brave is the daughter who tries to convince her Cuban parents to vote for *any* Clinton. "I can't vote for that man's wife," my mother told me after saying she was considering not voting at all. Many Cubans (my parents included) hate Bill Clinton for several reasons, the most relevant one in this instance being that he was president when the Elián González deportation saga occurred. The Clinton administration is, in the minds of many Cuban Americans of my parents' generation, solely to blame for the decision to send six-year-old González back to Cuba several months after he was rescued from a broken raft floating in the Florida Straits. Many speculate it cost Al Gore the election. In March 2000, then mayor Alex Penelas described Gore's connection to the decisions surrounding Elián as "guilt by association" and warned that

Miami's Cuban population would hold the Clinton administration responsible should González be sent back. He was right: In Florida, 81 percent of the Cubans voted for Bush in 2000. Many of those Cubans saw themselves in Elián, in his story, in his mother's wish to build what she hoped would be a better life for them in the United States. She drowned in the crossing.

Historically, much of this hatred originated with the Kennedy Administration, which many Cubans blame for the failure of the Bay of Pigs Invasion. This blame eventually translated into a general distrust of the Democratic Party—a feeling that was fading with voters my parents' age until Elián's deportation reinvigorated it, spawning a new generation of one-issue voters. (In December 2000, during my annual checkup while I was home from college, my doctor—a Cuban man in his early fifties—showed me a framed photo of a banner he and other men had hung off a Miami expressway overpass. It read, THANK YOU, ELIÁN. WE REMEMBERED IN NOVEMBER.)

Elián's deportation reignited that grudge, mobilizing Cuban Americans to go out and vote *against* Gore. This grudge, I learned from my mom and others, now extended to Hillary. Over the phone, I told her, "Mom, you *have* to vote for her, you can't *not* vote, it's too dangerous."

As light-skinned Cuban Americans based in Miami, we'd always had the privilege of being able to vote, perhaps in part because my parents' demographic historically tended to vote with the party currently most interested in voter suppression. My parents have never struggled to vote or to register to vote in all the time they've been American citizens—a privilege denied darker Americans since this country's beginnings, and which continues to this day. My own difficulties registering to vote only occurred when I moved to Tallahassee (where some supposed mix-up with my Social Security number got me temporarily kicked off the voter rolls), but this administrative hurdle was nothing compared to the extent of voter suppression impacting black and brown Americans. We had the privilege of not (yet) doubting whether or not we'd be allowed to vote, should we choose to do so.

"I can't believe Marco Rubio actually endorsed what's-his-face," my mom said, Trump having taken on Voldemort status for us. "I *hate* Marco Rubio now. He didn't show up for things because he was too busy running for president and then he gave *that* up. He didn't do his job."

"But *you* have to do *your* job," I said, skirting the cheesiness of that segue. She caught it, though, and made a farting sound with her mouth. When Obama was running for president, my sister and I both made calls on his behalf using the tools he provided on his website; we were using those skills, however rusty, on her, and she knew it.

I told her to think of a vote for Hillary Clinton as a vote for herself, for all the times in her life when a man with less experience or training ended up as her boss. I asked her to think of it as a vote for me, or for my sister—two women whose commitment to their careers had sometimes caused conflict with the men in their lives. I told her a story about my old job, how a more qualified woman had been passed over for department chair in favor of a man who'd once referred to her as "the old girl" in a department meeting—this happening while she was serving as assistant chair. I kept stories like this coming (any woman reading this and/or that you know has tons of them). I even asked her to think of a vote for Hillary as a vote for her forthcoming granddaughter (my sister was pregnant with her first kid, who we'd learned would be a girl). Imagine her being born while a woman was president, I said. I didn't care if this tactic was cheap; short of anything illegal, I did or said whatever it took to get her to go out and vote against Trump. I had no qualms about playing the gender card with her; besides, hadn't she been willing to vote for Marco Rubio out of similar allegiances? Isn't that the truest explanation as to how Rubio got just the tip?

As 2016 wore on, I heard from more and more friends back home that their parents weren't voting. We were afraid their apathy would translate into a Trump win. Our families didn't seem to recognize all the times in history—as recently as 2000—that their own votes *against* a candidate have been a crucial deciding factor. They didn't realize that not voting— the ultimate gesture of complacency—was a privilege they didn't actually have: It only felt that way because they lived in Miami, a place where it was easy to think, if you were Cuban, that you were white and therefore not part of the immigrant groups Trump was making a campaign out of promising to deport. It was a complacency that went against their very presence in the United States, a complacency they sometimes incorrectly attribute to Cubans still in Cuba or Cubans who left the island long after they did. All my friends and I did between then and that November was urge our parents not to stay home in protest on election day. That staying home was no protest at all, but a relinquishing of the very freedom their families had left Cuba hoping to restore. All we did was urge them to do what they already knew how to do in moments like that: make their disgust for a candidate known by voting instead for whichever candidate had the best shot at beating them.

II.

Less than a week after Trump won the 2016 election—including Florida, by a very slim margin—my sister gave birth to her daughter at Jackson Memorial Hospital in Miami. I'd booked a flight that had me in Miami seven days before and seven days after her due date, the hope being I'd be there even if the baby was early or late. She arrived nine days early, which means she was three days old when I met her. I spoke with my sister over the phone her first night as a mom, while she was still in the hospital. She was whispering because the baby was in the room with her. She told me the whole birth story and said that just after the all-woman staff helped her deliver a healthy baby girl, before they'd even cut the cord, the first thing my sister said to her daughter was, "Go back inside, Trump's the president."

Three days later, I met the girl whose impending arrival had helped me convince my mom that Hillary Clinton was the better role model for her new granddaughter. My timing was off for the official arrival of my niece, but I was home in Miami for another life-shifting event late that November: the death of Fidel Castro.

I am always somehow back in Miami when something monumental happens in our community: the first time Fidel supposedly died; Celia Cruz's death; Obama's 2015 visit to Cuba; the Elián González chaos. The events of the González ordeal all coincided with my breaks when I was home from college, a year of events that I had to turn into a novel in order to write through the media's inaccurate and incomplete portrayal of frenzied Cubans throwing themselves at the feet of a young boy-turned-symbol.

The first time Fidel Castro died was on my birthday in 2006. I'd been living in Minnesota but was in Miami when the announcement went out that Castro had had an operation and was temporarily ceding power to his brother. This being the first time ever that Castro had voluntarily stepped away from his dictatorship, speculation ran wild, and Miami Cubans took to the streets to celebrate the death of a tyrant, a symbol of terror and loss for exiled Cubans of all races and faiths. What better birthday present, my parents joked.

The morning after his latest death was confirmed, my

sister texted, "Fidel is dead . . . again," one of twenty-six messages from friends and relatives sharing the news. But I'd already heard—around midnight, Cubans of every age poured into the streets of Miami to celebrate the death of a dictator who'd had a profound effect on our lives, who was, in many ways, the reason we were here in the first place. I was in Westchester, a south Miami neighborhood that's arguably the heart of Miami's Cuban community (and as a Hialeah native, I'd be the first one to argue).

The news reports surrounding Castro's official final death showed you loud Cubans parading through the streets. It showed you shots of us hitting pots and pans and making much noise and yelling and crying and honking horns. It gave you familiar rehashed images of old men sipping café out of tiny cups outside Versailles. That was all part of it, yes, almost as if we'd rehearsed these predictable roles, the scripts all but handed to us. But the news didn't show you the more prevalent scenes: the tearful conversations happening between generations around café con leche that first morning without Fidel, the sun setting on one populist tyrant while rising over the specter of another, this one in the country we now called home. It didn't show you how, at a dinner with other Miami-based Latinx writers a couple of nights after the Miami Book Fair, we joked that Castro would never die because he is protected by powerful Santería. (The joke was also that reporters would take such a statement from us as fact because of our heritage.) It didn't show you how we bemoaned the inaccuracies and misinformation perpetuated by American writers and reporters who see Cuba as "material," how their vague efforts to bring attention to the island and its people are in actuality silencing them, because by telling their version of Cuba—a version white American audiences are receptive toward because the messenger often looks and sounds like them—they are replacing the island's true voices with their own. Those conversations weren't sexy and didn't involve us banging on pots and pans. Those conversations didn't make for good sound bites. Those conversations—like many of our current ones, which these days are more often than not triggered by our dictator-in-the-making's deranged tweets, a form that literally limits character count and thus traffics in sound bites—are hard to have, and so they have an equally hard time finding their way into the immediate coverage of the aftermaths of events. Plus, it doesn't sell papers, it doesn't get clicks, and those of us who want to write these harder, thornier responses are told by those in charge that there isn't room for nuance. From one night to the next, we learned that the dictator who'd served as a symbol of oppression our entire lives was finally gone. How do you sum up what this change might come to mean for a whole nation in a sound bite? The news cycle had long moved on by the time the new reality of this shift and all its complexities had sunk in.

Many of us out on the streets the night Castro died and the morning after were there as symbols, too. We were there as witnesses, as bearers of memory. Many of us were out

because we had family that couldn't be there—mothers, abue-
los, cousins who died at the hands of the Castro regime or
who haven't been allowed to leave. We were there to comfort
each other and to honor the sacrifices these family members
made. The morning after Castro died, in the house in Westchester, I awoke to stories I'd heard a thousand times being
told with more verve and energy than they'd been told in a
long while. We were calling each other around the city and
the country and saying, "I am thinking of you." I wondered
what it would be like for my niece to grow up with Castro
dead; she would only have his specter tugging at her sense of
Cubanidad. She would never know him as a living, breathing
force. What would she come to think of him, what would she
be taught, and what would she ignore? When I look to history,
it seems that whatever legacy Castro might hold for my niece
will almost certainly be overshadowed by the inevitable legacy made by the man elected president the week before she
was born an American.

I cannot speak for every Cuban or Cuban American and
have never embraced the chance to do so. I can only tell you
my reaction when I heard the news about Castro. I was already asleep when my partner, who is also Cuban, woke me
up and after he told me that Fidel Castro was dead, before
I was even fully awake, my eyes still closed, the first thing
I said was, "That's impossible, he'll never die." My reaction
came not from a place of rational thought, but instead was

grounded in a trained complacency regarding the state of Cuban politics: The rhetoric in the United States surrounding the country of my parents' birth was essentially always the same, and it had trained me from a young age to expect nothing, not even the most inevitable thing—Castro's death—even as we hoped its occurrence could someday bring about real change in our relations with the island. I just didn't believe, deep in my half-asleep heart, that he could die. Our collective half-asleep heart is the same place from which sprang the confidence many other Americans felt that Donald Trump would never be president. *No need to worry,* my friends living on the coasts told me before the primaries, he's not a real threat. Even the weekend before the election, sitting in an Indianapolis hotel lounge eating free appetizers with a friend who works in New York publishing and who'd flown out for the same conference—even then, when I told him we should prepare for the worst, he insisted there was nothing to worry about, that I was being alarmist. He was phenomenally confident. He ordered another drink.

We came in from the airport at different times, but we'd passed the same messages on the same billboards: THIS IS TRUMP COUNTRY!

The message was huge and unmissable from the freeway. It was extremely red. It instantly reminded me of the propaganda all over Cuba that I've only seen in photos: murals of a dictator that were designed to convince citizens that the coming regime was an inevitability. Murals that still stand as proof of how the fabric of any nation can be disastrously altered.

But it's just a billboard, my friend seemed to be telling me, already ignoring its meaning. It's not like it's a sign.

III.

When it comes to ignoring legitimate warnings, no one is better at it than the born-and-raised residents of Miami-Dade County when faced with the threat of a hurricane—one of several natural disasters we'll be seeing more and more of in the decades to come, whether we believe the signs or not.

My personal litmus test for whether or not someone is a legit Miamian is based almost entirely on their response to a hurricane warning. If they evacuate any sooner than when the water is waist deep, Miami might be where they *live*, but it's not where they're *from*. Sincere and complete disbelief in a hurricane's ability to hit your neighborhood is as Miami as getting your cafecito and croquetas from a ventanita: The former is a state of mind that can't be appropriated the way the latter has, because we are raised not to take a storm's threat seriously. I have fallen for and perpetuated the hype that when it comes to hurricanes, we are as invincible as Fidel once seemed. It'll turn at the last minute, there's no reason to cancel school, this is just a way for supermarkets to make money—all things I've heard and even said, waiting for hurricanes in Miami.

We wait to put up the shutters until the last minute because it's a pain to take them off later once the storm makes that last-minute turn away from us, so we don't take them off—not all of them—and that means one room in the house will be dark for weeks, maybe months. We watch from our still-electrified homes as the storm instead devastates the countries our families are from and maybe still live in, our batteries and bottles of water all suddenly in the wrong place. We wonder how much warning they had, if somehow the *condition* of being warned—even when ignored—is in any way the key to avoiding disaster, as if the National Hurricane Center were casting protective spells instead of predicting possible storm paths. The bigger the warning, the more powerful the privileges behind it, the more powerful the force-field, and so the more radical the inevitable turn the storm takes away from us. In our faulty memories, it happens that way every time.

Hurricane Andrew did not turn. Our shutters went up at the last minute, my father putting them on only after having done the same at the houses of both sets of grandparents. None of us evacuated because no one told us we needed to evacuate. We wouldn't have anyway. My parents' pride in our home meant they would go down with it. They didn't want to ride out the storm in the closest shelter—the local middle school—because really, how bad could it be? It's just rain and wind. We had plastic jugs of water. We'd filled up the bathtub, put the freezer on the highest setting. We were extra prepared—my dad was an electrician and so we even had a portable generator.

We spent the whole storm huddled in our bathroom, hearing branches and carports snap and tumble outside, hearing thunder but not seeing any lightning flashes because of the shutters. Rain so hard it didn't sound like rain, but like someone continuously raking something metal—I imagined the bottom of a giant bucket—against the roof. I remember darkness and my mother trying to convince my father not to go outside to see what was happening. I don't remember if he did or not. After, I remember the mess, the way every leaf and palm frond for miles plastered the streets and driveways. I remember how the cleaning and repairing felt impossible and like it would last forever. We didn't know where to start, but it almost didn't matter, as long as we started somewhere.

We were north of the worst damage from that storm. Two weeks after the academic year was supposed to have started, I walked into middle school for the first time to find our classes overcrowded with kids from "down south," as we said, kids from maybe fifteen miles away, their own schools completely destroyed so they'd been reassigned to ours for the whole year while theirs got rebuilt. These kids hated us and our teachers and our still-standing school buildings, so we hated them back. We were all too young to understand the magnitude of what had been lost, so we took it out on each other. We fought over who did or didn't belong there instead of moving in the same general direction toward healing. This was how we started sixth grade.

In Miami-Dade County, building codes were strengthened after entire communities were literally blown away by Hurricane Andrew. We learned good lessons too late. Shutters remained up and rooms in our houses stayed dark as penance. Some of the lessons stuck: The house my sister bought came with impact windows rated up to 150 mph winds. But when a coming storm's winds reportedly exceed that limit, she still doesn't put up shutters. She banks on the storm losing strength as it approaches, a real Miami move. For Hurricane Irma in September 2017—the first storm she'd weather in that house—she didn't evacuate, despite her home being in a recommended evacuation zone and despite having my niece, who was by then ten months old. She didn't go to my parents' house either; they are farther inland, but she told me she didn't want to ride out Irma there because their house would be dark from the shutters they'd likely put up at the last minute. She wanted to see for herself what was coming.

I watched from across the country as Irma strengthened. I read tweets from the National Hurricane Center saying that the storm's size and strength left them utterly speechless. New trajectories showed that it didn't matter which way the storm turned, it would no doubt hit them. I lost my Miami-born-and-bred resolve and sent frantic texts to my sister saying she should reconsider her choice not to evacuate. She assured me that she and her husband were prepared, she just needed to pick up baby yogurt and steak. The year before, I'd missed her baby shower in October when the threat of a hurricane headed to Florida canceled my connecting flight into Miami. My family thought I should've gone for it, that the worst-case scenario was that I'd have to turn back in Atlanta. "No," I told them when I broke the news I wouldn't make it, "the worst-case scenario is that I get stuck in Miami as a hurricane hits and I can't get back to Nebraska, where I actually live now." This scenario didn't register for them as a possibility. They said, "You know it's gonna turn like it always does." In that case, they were right, and they're still annoyed I missed the baby shower, that I didn't make the airline fly me toward the storm. That I let my practicality and realism influence my choices.

In the days before Irma made landfall, I was giving a talk at a liberal arts college in Washington State, the entire campus cloaked in thick smoke from raging wildfires—another disaster. Local authorities asked that we avoid going outside, as the air was hazardous. I went outside anyway, because it was time for the campus tour my hosts had planned for me. I wasn't taking the threat seriously; I'm just like my sister.

Hurricane Irma did not turn. And so *It's not really coming* morphed into *It's not going to be that bad.* In eastern Washington, within hours of landing, I turned off the storm coverage on my hotel's TV and went to a rally in support of DACA

(Deferred Action for Childhood Arrivals), the reality of its end still sitting like a glacier inside me; then Attorney General Jeff Sessions had announced the Trump regime's repeal of DACA the day before. Some rally attendees wore face masks or bandanas over their noses and mouths to protect them from the smoke. I had no such protection, didn't think it was that bad to warrant the search for any. On the walk there, I texted my sister to start driving to Nebraska, that they could still make it with plenty of time, that I had an awesome basement, so she should bring our mom and dad, too. "Relax, don't give in to panic," she wrote back twenty minutes later. Why does the worst have to happen for us to believe it could happen at all? I thought of those Indiana billboards announcing the kind of country we now live in. How big do the signs have to be before we take the warnings seriously? How many years do the murals have to be up before we can see them anew as symbols for what has already been lost? How long before we realize that our own inaction—our own complacency, our own silence—is at the root of every disaster we watch unfold? These questions are no longer rhetorical. Our answers depend on how immediate the threat to our survival feels, and for many of us, the immediacy of that threat has already mobilized us toward revolutionary action. And then there are those of us who can keep ignoring the signs, for now. Right up until we take our next breath and realize just how long we've been inhaling the ash along with the air.

■

The smoke in Washington State was there for a while; they get less rain than they used to. It's hotter, too—good for the wine industry, I was told on the tour. A silver lining, the guide said, it's getting too hot for grapes in California now. I hear in that forecast a different version of *It's not going to be that bad*. At least it's an acknowledgment of our new not-normal, this era brought on by our very denial that the storms were on their way. The very least we can do now is accept that the disaster is here, but the fastest way to guarantee our peril is to do nothing in the face of it. No matter how dark it leaves the house, it's time to put up the shutters. Take a deep breath and notice what you taste; no matter how uncomfortable it feels, it's time to put on the face masks. In fact, it's already too late.

III

RESISTANCE
IN ACTION

EASE OF EXIT

MY PARENTS THREW ME A SURPRISE PARTY when I graduated from college. As the first person in my family to do so, it was in many ways a party for all of us, which is why they rented out a banquet hall—the same one in which several friends and cousins had held their quinceañeras years earlier. (Not me, though, as I didn't have a quinceañera, which I suspect is partly why my parents threw me such an elaborate college graduation party.) They'd told me we were headed to a baby shower for a different cousin, this one a year older than me and recently married. They'd even made a fake invitation for the fake event, had tacked it up to the fridge for me to find.

In a move reminiscent of *Sesame Street*'s "This Is Your Life" segment (the one hosted by a Muppet named Guy Smiley), my parents had packed Las Delicias Banquet Hall in Hialeah with everyone they felt had played a key part in me arriving at that moment, whether I knew them or not. Shortly after everyone yelled "Surprise!" my dad took the microphone and started the festivities by introducing one of the few white American families there.

"Do you recognize these people?" he asked, pointing to them.

I did not.

"Those are the people who sold us our house. Because we lived in that house, you went to the schools you went to, had the teachers you had, everything. We would not be standing here today had they never sold us the house."

The family waved from their table.

This sentiment, that a house is so much more than a house, that a house creates your destiny, shapes your fate, has played out in various ways throughout my life. My parents still live in that house even though my sister and I have long since moved out. When my dad paid it off while I was in high school, he celebrated by burning various mortgage-related documents over a charcoal grill in the backyard. He made us all come outside to watch. Within no time, he would decide to borrow against the house in order to help me pay for college.

While I was married, I saved for a house, the word *house* being synonymous with future, with family. Marriage plopped me into a comforting, recognizable narrative: You save for a wedding, you have the wedding; you save for a house, you buy the house; you save for a baby, etc. For the first time in my life, I felt like I knew what I was supposed to be doing, and everyone around me seemed to be on board. But when I finally bought a house—in Tallahassee, Florida, the closing coming a month shy of my thirtieth birthday—my dad made an ominous pronouncement: "You guys aren't house people. You are condo people." I took this as an insult; he was saying we weren't the kind of couple who liked to work on things. Now I understand his judgment as an indictment of a marriage that he sensed was destined to fail.

The house in Tallahassee came with a cautionary tale. I bought it from a lawyer who'd been gifted the house as a wedding present from his parents, who just so happened to live in the much bigger house next door. For reasons that were never made clear but about which the town's real estate agents loved to speculate, the house had been on the market for more than a year, the rumor being that the seller's father (also a lawyer, powerful and well known in the community, famous in part for being fired by Ted Bundy) had put out a warning that no one should buy it. I was moving there from Los Angeles; his warning hadn't made it that far.

Everyone who came to work on the house had a story about it. One contractor told me that when the previous owners had put up the FOR SALE sign (something they did without consulting the givers of this wedding present of a house), the seller's mother came over with a Sharpie and defaced it, scrawling AT THE COST OF OUR LOVE or some such pronouncement across it. The seller's father would occasionally knock on my door and ask after the baby, forgetting over and over again that I did not have children. He would look past me into the living room with a scowl on his face that read, *Then why do you need all this space?*

And he was right; with that house came expectations. There was a room that the real estate agent said had been a nursery and *boom*, now it was the nursery forever. The first year we lived there, we left it mostly unfurnished, not really acknowledging why. The room seemed to be waiting for someone else. When the marriage ended and the house was sold, with it went everything the house was supposed to become. I'd written a novel in a bright office in that house, but it's the empty never-our-nursery that haunted me when I moved to Lincoln, single and singing the praises of renting forever.

That is, until Carol intervened. A financial planner, she'd been recommended to me by my accountant, who sensed from my shoebox of receipts and my tendency to bring every official-looking paper I got in the mail to our meetings that I needed some financial guidance.

Carol was in her late fifties and about a foot taller than me. She had a wide smile and a big office that suggested she likely ran the place. (I'd later learn that, yes, she did.) On her desk sat monogrammed coasters that probably weighed a couple of pounds each. She was originally from Mitchell, South Dakota. I'd once been to Mitchell's famed Corn Palace. We hit it off instantly.

"First things first," Carol said after reviewing the financials of my life, "you need to buy some property. In Lincoln, that probably means a house."

I did what anyone under thirty-five does in a moment like that, I pulled out my phone and tweeted, "Someone tell me if I should buy a house?" Among the immediate responses was a direct message from my former husband, who I hadn't heard from in months: "no you should not buy a house. condo, though, maybe. just my 2€" [sic].

For the first time in my life, I had a stable income, no debt, and no financial dependents. (Despite my former husband valuing his own opinion highly enough to convert his proverbial two cents into euros, I'd been the primary earner in the marriage for the last six of its eight years, and we'd lived solely off my salary its final four.) I'd just sold my first house. I knew I was very lucky and that I was supposed to do something responsible with this privilege. I looked up from the incoming responses on my phone and said, "I'm not the homeowner type. Can I buy a Tesla instead?"

She nudged me away from the Tesla more gently than I deserved by saying I should wait on that "at least until Nebraska does a little better with the charging stations." I asked if I could buy a condo or a loft, or maybe a warehouse and live in that instead. I said I wanted to be able to roller-skate inside of whatever property I owned. I was an artist-type, I explained, and I had no problem with, say, a toilet out in the open. I had very cool poet friends out in Los Angeles doing exactly this, so yes, a warehouse would be perfect.

Carol was writing all of this down—the first of many indications that she was taking me seriously in a way I had not yet learned to do for myself. She looked up from her notepad and said, "Yeah, I *see* all this, but it's just not going to work in Lincoln. I'd say we've got another twenty or thirty years before we're a funky enough city to support warehouse living."

I joked that I'd likely be dead by then and showed her the Twitter replies on my phone, including the DM. We'd become fast friends. "From everything I'm putting together about you," she said, "it sounds like your number one priority with a property is actually what I'd call *ease of exit*. You want to be able to get out of something quickly if you need to. In Lincoln, that's a single-family home, close in town, one with some history to it, some charm. Condos in Lincoln don't move nearly as fast as houses," she said, more to my phone than to my face. "You really should consider a house."

"But that's not for me," I argued. Homes are for families. Homes are destiny. Homes determine everything from where your kids might go to college to how long your marriage will last. I was sitting in her office half-worrying I'd forgotten to brush my teeth that morning, wearing floral pajama pants and a cropped T-shirt that said TEAM GG and had sketches of all four Golden Girls across my boobs. I was single and a woman and had been told by my own father that I was a condo person. I did not, in my estimation, radiate house-worthiness.

She fanned the pages of a file with my name on it out in front of her and said, "Jennine, houses are for people who can afford houses."

It took almost a year for Carol to help me rewrite the narrative that had been keeping me from buying a home. It's a pervasive narrative, one that recasts home ownership not as a stable, smart investment, but as a symbol of a kind of commitment, or the epitome of the American Dream—one you're only entitled to once you're legally married and/or en route to growing a family. In the house I would eventually buy, I stood next to my real estate agent in its bathroom and freaked out at the sight of an oversized custom tub from 1939, which, with its built-in seats, looked perfect for bathing a couple of toddlers. I shook my head *no* and said, "I can't buy this house. A family deserves this place. I see *kids* in this tub!"

She shrugged. "That's weird. I see a great tub."

And later, when we sat down in the kitchen's breakfast nook to write out the offer and I stopped cold after picturing not myself but a faceless family sitting there with their bowls of cereal, she said, "Think of this as a bank you can live in."

Both my real estate agent and Carol were teaching me to see and think of owning property differently, not as a symbol but as an investment, one that everything about my financial life said I'd earned. They were teaching me how to see a house as *equity*, a word that, like *escrow*, I'd misunderstood for too long. (I still don't know what escrow is; I like to imagine it's what my grandmother would say in Spanglish were she trying to call my attention to a large black bird.) And while I could fall in love with a space, I was also learning that every corner need not be imbued with meaning. A house is, ultimately, just a house—a building. The one I bought happens to have four bedrooms. When I moved in and an older woman living across the street asked me, after learning I didn't have children, what I was doing with all the space, I said, "Pretty much whatever I want."

I met with Carol again post-closing to update her on the purchase. I brought many papers she did not need to see. She said the next thing I needed to do was get a will. I said, "No thanks!" Then she very calmly, and with her typical wisdom, explained why I was being ridiculous. She was teaching me again, this time to accept the life I'd built, to recognize it as stable and worth protecting. She sent me a follow-up email with links.

That email is still marked as unread in my inbox, because a week later, I got another email stating that Carol had passed away unexpectedly. It was impersonal, bcc'd to me from someone I'd never met at Carol's firm. The email's third sentence stated that "the firm is prepared to partner with you and to continue serving your wealth management needs."

I wrote back asking about a memorial service, but it was Carol I wanted to reply to—after learning not from that email but from her obituary about the myriad boards she sat on and the millions of dollars she raised for various Lincoln causes: the Nebraska Humanities Council, the YMCA, the Spring Creek Prairie Audubon Center. Her obituary says that she was a Tab addict who perhaps single-handedly "kept the company in business . . . buying dozens of twelve-packs at a time." I had so many new questions for her, about what really mattered, about what versions of wealth really needed managing. I wanted to know how she'd gotten hooked on Tab. I wanted to know what it was like to grow up in Mitchell, if she actually hated how the Corn Palace was the most famous thing about her hometown. I wanted desperately to know who else had loved her, if anyone had been by her side when she'd died, if there was someone I could call to say I was sorry she was gone. I wanted to know her address.

■

When my email asking about a memorial service went unanswered, I again did what anyone under thirty-five does: I googled her, gathering every fact I could about her life like a bird building a nest. This act led to even more questions not just about her and her life, but about another, stranger element to our relationship: Why was she so set on helping me map out my financial life when, for the vast majority of our relationship, I wasn't technically her client? In the eighteen months we worked together, as our scheduled hour-long meetings turned into three-hour-long conversations over coffee—conversations that I admittedly used as a kind of free therapy—I'd opened no accounts with her firm. Carol made exactly zero dollars off of me. It's a truth I've been avoiding because I still can't make sense of it. Someone who knew so much about maximizing returns on investments wasted a lot of time listening to my stories about everything from the lackluster Lincoln dating scene to the epic journey of how my family became an American one. Even more bizarrely, exactly three weeks before she died, I finally did open an account, with a check for the whopping amount of two hundred dollars. "Go crazy," I'd joked as I'd pushed the check across her lacquered desk. I'd written it out right in front of her, had wanted to start the account with more, but she *advised me against that.* She said she had a feeling, based on the time of year it was, that we should hold off on any bigger moves. Small as the amount was, I was relieved to have finally opened an account because it made me feel less guilty. She'd spent so much time advising me for no financial return whatsoever, and the opening of an account meant maybe that would change, would give her a return on her investment in me.

I eventually learned from the internet that there would be

a memorial service. Like white American weddings, I'd only been to two white American funerals that I remember. One was when I was in ninth grade, for a teacher who'd died of a heart attack while I was her student. The other was for my mother-in-law. Like the white American weddings, at both funerals a program was given out. I've been to maybe a dozen Cuban funerals and have never been handed a program or sat through any eulogies. We do things differently in Miami: Within hours of someone dying, we head to Vista Memorial Gardens, where there's an open casket (containing the relative we more than likely watched die) at one end of a room filled with couches and flowers. The viewing lasts about twenty-four hours, with people coming and going and coming again, usually leaving to grab Cuban sandwiches or croquetas, always returning with greasy white bags, leftovers for those of us who stayed behind to greet newcomers. The sobbing and laughter ebb and flow like waves. Kids run around playing and everyone is grateful for the distraction. People show up, and at the other end of the room, sinking into a couch, other people hiss, *What is he even doing here?* Sometimes there's an argument that everyone's been expecting for decades. You stay as long as you want or need, and so sometimes that means you sleep on one of those couches, because you know this is the last time you'll see the deceased's physical body, and that knowledge compels you—especially if it's your mother or father who died—to stay put until the casket gets shut. I've gone home to get pillows for my parents when their parents died. I've seen coolers filled with beers in the shadows of open trunks of Buicks parked in the funeral home's lot. I've had friends from high school who'd been out of touch for years show up straight from work—new kids in tow and still in their daycare uniforms—because they'd seen my grandma's Facebook page turn into a memorial. I've seen ex-boyfriends looking for an excuse to say hi, asking why my husband wasn't there. I've seen half the men under fifty leave the room to go look at someone's new car. There is no official start time to our funerals; the only official time comes when the viewing period ends, which is when the casket gets moved from the room you've called home to a wall (because being buried in the ground is much more expensive, so no one in my family has opted for that yet). The experience of a Cuban funeral in Miami is chaotic and cathartic and nothing like the two American funerals I've attended.

I was initially hesitant to go to Carol's memorial service until one of her best friends reached out to me, telling me Carol had my first two books "ready to take along for reading on her upcoming trip to Maine, which was scheduled for the weekend after her accident." Because I imagined the kind of understandably somber event I'd been to in the past, I worried it would be intimate enough that my presence would be a disruption. A Cuban funeral is, in some ways, all disruption; if a stranger were to walk in and hang out in the room, we'd probably never realize it.

Even though the announcement online had called it "A

Celebration of Life," I still hadn't anticipated it to be festive. So I was confused when her husband, stationing himself at the entrance's double doors, greeted everyone with a warm smile while sporting khaki shorts and a Hawaiian shirt. I was in black slacks and a loose-fitting dark-gray blouse. He shook my hand and thanked me for coming, and that's when I realized that dance music was playing in the banquet hall behind him, and that many of the people there—the ones who'd likely known Carol much better than I had—were similarly dressed as if for a backyard barbeque.

The room was a bigger and higher-ceilinged version of Las Delicias Banquet Hall in Hialeah. There was a cash bar, which meant drinking while grieving was not considered shameful or weak here; no one was hiding their booze in the parking lot. No couches or rows of seats; instead, there were dozens of round tables set up just like for a quinceañera. There was no casket anchoring the room, either. Carol's ashes were in a lovely polished wooden box, her name engraved on a gold plate affixed to its lid, the box surrounded by pictures of her posed with those who loved her most, the box and pictures set up on a table off to the side of a dance floor. Oh my god, would there be dancing? Were these white people going to defy my every preconceived notion about how white people grieve and spend the evening dancing in front of Carol's ashes? Dancing at a funeral seemed even too Cuban for Cubans.

"I am really uncomfortable," my date said. (Yes, I'd brought a date to the service, don't judge me. I'd asked my boyfriend to come with me because I fully expected to be the only person of color there—and we were, aside from myself, my boyfriend, a mixed-race child, and a Southeast Asian man, despite there being maybe three hundred people in attendance.) I grabbed his hand and walked us over to the main table. The biggest photo on it was Carol's wedding photo. She's standing alone, bouquet held with both hands at her waist, a large white hat like an oversized halo on her head. It was more elegant than a quinces photo (no long fake nails, no pearl-and-crystal-bedazzled crown, no tacky fan splayed open across layers of tulle hiding a hoop skirt—I am, of course, describing my own quinces photo here; though I didn't have the party, my parents did have me pose for formal quinces portraits) and it hit me that Carol had just turned sixty, an age that, should I ever reach it, I plan on celebrating with the formal quinces party I never had, but times four—my Quadruple Quinceañera.

Near the bar sat a long table loaded with food. I'd later learn that everything on it was something Carol was famous for making or that she'd loved eating. Carol and her husband were big on entertaining and threw epic parties with amazing food. People kept talking about her pinwheels.

Eventually, there were eulogies—all but one of them given by men she'd worked with, men who all mentioned, repeatedly, that even though Carol was never a mother, she was like a mom to them—and there was a slide show. Every ten or so photos were of Tab: cases of Tab, Carol double fisting Tab, pickup beds full of Tab. She'd been hooked since she was fourteen. The service ended with a Tab toast in Carol's honor, with everyone getting a small cup of this soda Carol had loved that I'd never even tried. They planned for two hundred people. They ran out of cups.

■

At the memorial service, a male coworker had given a eulogy where he said Carol was the only Democrat in the office. Everyone sort of laughed, like this was some inside joke. He announced he was a Republican and for a few moments hijacked the funeral with stories that I'm sure in his mind were about Carol, but were really about him. A week later I learned that he was the person to whom my account had been reassigned.

Over email, I wrote a long message carefully detailing my objections, which included an all caps line of I WILL NEVER AGAIN LET ANY MAN TELL ME WHAT TO DO WITH MY LIVELIHOOD. Then I deleted all that and said simply that I'd prefer to work with a woman.

The company's response informed me that there wasn't a single other female financial advisor in their office. Carol had been the only one. This was shameful, and when I next met with someone in person, I asked when they would be hiring a woman, or better yet, several women. I was told they had no plans to do so, and that they could maybe find a woman in Omaha. I thought about how every man who Carol had worked with who'd spoken at her service had felt the need to define her by what she *hadn't* done, which was reproduce—how limited it revealed their imaginations to be when it came to a woman's potential; how the qualities Carol demonstrated that I most benefitted from—her easy confidence, her humor and grace, her earnestness and generosity—weren't necessarily ones that seemed to count on paper.

I closed my account there within the month. I am still looking for a woman's help. And I still live in the house Carol told me to buy.

Like Carol in that office, my house stands out almost comically, a historic two-story Tudor in a sea of midcentury ranch houses all built two decades later and over the same handful of years. Everyone who comes to work on the house has a story about it: Back in the day, it was the only house for miles, and all the land surrounding it—where everyone else's homes now stand—was a ranch owned by the people who built it. "Well, well, this was a Taylor family home," the inspector said, referring to some Lincoln royalty for which I had no context as he shined a flashlight on some piece of metal in the attic. Someone had, in 1938 or so, scrawled the words *Taylor Project* on it before installing it. A carpenter informed me that based on the year the house was built and on something he saw happening structurally underneath a staircase, the basement was likely dug out by hand. Architecturally, the house makes no sense in the neighborhood; without this house, there wouldn't be a neighborhood. My real estate agent assures me I could sell it in a heartbeat.

What finally sold me on the house was not the custom

antique tub (though it is an amazing tub), but the fact that so many of the rooms were already painted teal—a color that makes me think of home. I live in it with a man I love who, like me, grew up in Miami, and because he is also a writer, the four bedrooms get put to use. We each have a study to write in, and the extra room is filled floor-to-ceiling with a couple thousand books. It's a library and a guestroom, and to our surprise and delight, we have visitors often enough that we have them sign a guestbook; we want a record of the fates this house might nudge.

Last summer, we planted a garden and put the tomatoes way too close together; we made notes for next year. Last fall, to save money, we sanded, stained, and painted the new staircase the carpenter built when the original one wore out. And last winter, our heating bill was outrageous because we kept the house Florida-warm.

We call the place the Miami Embassy. For now, it's home.

IMAGINE ME HERE, OR HOW I BECAME A PROFESSOR

THE SHORT ANSWER IS: BY ACCIDENT. THAT'S what I usually say, the quickest version of the story I tell most often when asked. Then I double down, and more self-effacing garbage spills out: *I had no idea what I was doing when I applied for my first tenure-track job and I didn't even know what I was getting myself into because I sort of applied for that job on a whim and I guess I somehow tricked* *a school into hiring me HA HA HA HA.* No one ever questions this version, despite the fact that applying to academic jobs is so time consuming and requires such a big emotional and financial investment that saying I did it "on a whim" should be a huge red flag to anyone who knows better.

Here's the clear, technical answer to the question "How did I become a professor?"—which I'm laying out here because there was a good chunk of my adult life when I didn't know the answer despite having successfully completed college and graduate school: I got a bachelor's degree, then I got a graduate degree (an MFA in creative writing), and I worked a bunch of odd jobs while writing my first book. These included after-school daycare provider, movie projectionist, standardized test scorer, college access counselor, personal assistant to a douchebag (this was in Los Angeles, though douchebags exist everywhere), and, ever so briefly, search engine optimization . . . person. (I don't know what my official title was: I looked at a website all day and made lists of keywords and it was incredibly boring.) Once my first book was published and getting some good attention, I applied to a tenure-track assistant professor job in my home state of Florida after googling "What is a dossier?" When I got that job I knew almost right away it wasn't a good fit for me culturally, but I used my time there to learn and teach as much as I could in the hopes of figuring out if a life in academia was for me.

There's one part of my "By Accident" version that's fairly accurate: I didn't really know what I was doing my first time trying to land an academic job when it came to the actual *process* (hence the googling). I'd been out of graduate school for four years by then, but even while enrolled, I'd had very little guidance on what everyone kept calling "the market" (when you hear an academic using this term, most likely they are not talking about stocks—assuming they aren't in economics).

I had loved teaching while in grad school. The biggest reason why I hadn't pursued teaching immediately after was because I knew that, without a book, my options were limited when it came to teaching at the college level *and* making a living wage, so in the years prior to publishing my first collection of stories, I opted for more stable jobs that paid better than adjuncting and that—despite their regular hours (in fact, *because* of their regularity)—left me more time and energy to write.

Also, I'd heard stories from writer friends with credentials far more stunning than mine about how impossible it was to land a tenure-track position as a creative writer, so I figured, why even try? That was another big hurdle to pursuing a teaching position: this idea that it was impossible, that my work wasn't good enough to get me past even the first round of a search committee's screening.

Here's another hurdle, also rooted in insecurity: I'm a first-generation college student, and the idea of becoming a professor—one of those people who seemed to emanate brilliance and poise, the people who *made knowledge!*—felt like too big of a leap for me, as someone who comes from a working-class family of electricians. Add to this hurdle the fact that the vast majority of my professors were white, and that most of them were male, and that most of the books they taught and deemed important enough to be covered in survey courses were written by straight white men, and you can see how a Cuban girl from Miami could come to think academia wasn't the place for her.

■

There was a time, though, when I thought I could do almost anything. Growing up in the 1990s in Miami, I saw Cubans working as doctors, police officers, and teachers. Cubans were educated professionals in positions of authority everywhere in Miami-Dade County. As naive as it sounds, it took leaving Miami to realize that this wasn't the case everywhere—that not everyone knew a Cuban pediatrician or a Cuban lawyer. In essence, it took me leaving Miami to realize that I was not white.

The writer Carlos Eire, a Cuban exile who came to the United States in the Peter Pan flights in the early 1960s, makes a similar claim about losing his whiteness—though for him it's when he leaves Cuba—in his entertaining and often ridiculous "memoir." (The quotes are for the memoir's substantial falsehoods, which were brought to light after its publication and National Book Award win, and which later editions recount in a postscript buried at the very back, where readers often miss it. When I teach Cuban American literature and include this text, I have my students do a close reading of this postscript to learn how easy it is to use words to bury the truth, even when we purport to be correcting for it; I'm always tempted to have them rip it out and glue it on a page in the front, where it belongs.) He says "that it would take only one brief plane ride to turn [him] from a white boy into a spic." Here's the thing: In time, he would've been white again had he stayed in Miami instead of being sent to the Midwest. The version of the city that made me—where Spanish is spoken as much as English, where I grew up under the care and guidance of Cuban health professionals, school principals, and legislators—was, and to a large degree still is, a city that centers the Cuban American experience. Which means in Miami, eventually, we were the whites.

More proof I considered myself white: Going off to college, it did not occur to me before I left that there wouldn't be very many Latinx students on campus. Of course, back then, I wasn't saying Latinx. I wasn't saying Latina or Hispanic either. I was saying Cuban, because I thought every place was like the one in which I was raised, where distinctions about country of origin were extremely significant and thus were never, ever erased. But if I'd only counted Cubans on my campus, the number would've been even more discouraging. In college I became Latinx to find community, to survive. Except it's an identity category my parents refuse—they find it so broad as to be useless. Because of course a Cuban is not the same as a Puerto Rican, who is not the same as a Dominican, who is not the same as a Mexican, a Venezuelan, a Salvadoran, a Nicaraguan, a Guatemalan; to my parents, *Latino/a/x* is a white word, an imposed label that makes no sense to use somewhere like Miami. Whenever I fly home and hit Florida airspace, I imagine some form somewhere with my name on it, and after my name is the phrase *Hispanic/Latino*. As we move south, that phrase disappears *Harry Potter*–style and gets replaced by *Cuban*. This back-and-forth, and the friction it causes, marks my holidays, my trips to see my family, my fiction, my sense of who I am. It's productive and painful.

If you'd asked seventeen-year-old Jennine what percentage of her college's student population was Cuban, she would've, no joke, said probably 25 or 30 percent, but she would've really thought it was closer to 40 percent and just known not to say that lest it come off as arrogant—because some Cubans *are* arrogant about the tremendous successes many of us have had in this country. Back then, I thought we ran everything.

The fact that I never even thought to check my school's demographics until after I'd committed to going there also proves I was a version of white: I didn't even think about race on my campus before getting there, didn't even know how or why it mattered. Another white giveaway: The reality of those numbers, when I finally learned them, shocked me.

■

In the fall of 2017, while speaking at a predominantly white college in the American South about my novel, *Make Your*

Home Among Strangers, I asked several hundred students gathered in an assembly to count how many professors they'd had (or would have) who looked like them.

Think about it: A person typically has maybe four professors a semester, two semesters a year (more if your school uses the quarter system). You're in college for four years, maybe five if you run into some institutional or personal snags. How many professors did you have with whom you shared various easily recognizable identity categories: your race, your ethnicity, your gender identity, your physical ability? How many times did you see a version of yourself in charge of your learning community?

I let the question sink in. Based on their shrugs and squints, the white male students thought it an odd question. So did many of the white women. More than ten, I asked? More than twenty?

Now most students in the room were nodding, though still shrugging, indicating they'd never really thought about it, they weren't sure what I was asking. The Black and Latinx and Asian and Arab students knew their answers immediately: one, maybe two.

I asked them all to think about what a wide divide there was between a response of "one or two" and "thirty," and if this seemed equitable. I pointed out that the relevant research is fairly conclusive: When college students see professors who look like them, they are more likely to stay in college, to graduate. This fact is partly why the visibility of first-gen professors has become so crucial: It's an identity category that isn't visible, and so we must work to make it one.

Eventually a white male student came to the microphone to ask what he specifically could do to fight what he'd just realized was a deeply unfair system. It was clear to me that he was shocked he hadn't before recognized this obvious privilege, and he genuinely wanted to mobilize it now in order to make his campus more inclusive. I made the suggestion that, given that this particular school would only have three new hires a year for the next five years (a fact I'd learned earlier in my visit), he should work with other students to demand that the school's administration guarantee that at least two-thirds of those hires be scholars of color. I also said that because of how the tenure system works (once you earn tenure, you are all but guaranteed a position at the school for life, which is why these jobs are all the rarer and part of why academic faculties have remained so overwhelmingly white), this solution would only be truly equitable if the hires were *all* scholars of color. That's the real solution, if you're genuinely serious about righting this wrong.

A young white woman in the front row, who'd neglected to raise her hand, called from her seat toward me on stage, "But that's racist." Her arms were crossed over her chest, her legs crossed, the hanging foot frantic at the ankle.

I placed my hands on the podium (to keep from moving them while I talked, an innocuous holdover from growing up Cuban in Miami that's sometimes read by white people as "aggressive" or "fierce" and by affluent people as "trashy," so I've learned to keep it in check in certain situations). I asked her what she would call the de facto system currently in place, the one that's led her college to have a faculty that is almost entirely white. "Isn't *that* system racist?" I asked.

She ignored my question and called me spiteful, said, "You don't know what you're talking about," an evaluation she tossed off after having sat through an hour-long presentation about the impact of inequality on a person's sense of their own humanity. An evaluation that triggered the kinds of insecurities planted in me and designed to keep me from ever getting to that podium in the first place. I quickly reminded myself that she was likely a first-year student at the school, in her third week of her college career. I was a tenure-track professor of Ethnic Studies and English at a major research university, invited to her campus because of my most recent book. What I mean is: It's safe to say I was closer to an expert on this topic than she was, but of the two of us, I was the only one who recognized this. What I mean is: I still had to remind myself that I had the training and the authority to be right.

She said, "The pendulum can't swing the other way."

And I said, "A pendulum analogy doesn't actually apply to this," but before I could elaborate, she started to cry, saying, "You're wrong. That's so wrong," as she wiped her face with the heel of her hand, everyone watching her as the tears flowed and soon grew out of her control—her chin trembling as she raised her voice in both volume and pitch. And then I remembered a former colleague of mine, a Chicanx historian tasked (along with me and other Latinx faculty) with figuring out why that school had such an exceptionally poor retention rate when it came to Latinx faculty, how in one tense meeting with various white administrators, he leaned my way and whispered, "There is no more precious commodity than a white woman's tears."

I said to the student, "Of course you feel that way, you are white. Doing the right thing is going to seem like unfairness to you." She'd been benefiting from this system her whole life and could not yet see it. For her and for many of us, the inherent unfairness of the white-dominated culture we live in is so prevalent as to appear naturally occurring. Any meaningful correction to this system would seem like it was going out of its way to benefit people of color, which it would— because that's what a systemic solution to a systemic problem requires.

She continued to talk over me as I spoke, her arms crossed, her legs crossed, foot jumping—all I heard as I tried to keep talking were the words *spite* and *spiteful*. And so I stopped explaining and let my hands go. I said, "You know what? Let's be real. Your school won't do this. You can relax. You have nothing to worry about."

The auditorium was suddenly very quiet, the other professors and administrators sitting up at so raw a truth falling out of my mouth. As a reflex I looked to the people of color in the room, to gauge if I should say what I really wanted to say.

There were young women who could've been me in this room, and I wanted their experiences centered in this conversation for once. It could change what they chose to major in, how much more quickly they would get to that podium after me someday. They were leaning forward, unblinking, waiting.

I continued to address their classmate, "As long as there are enough students who think like you do right now, you don't have to worry about people like me trying to teach you anything, okay? Don't you worry. *You'll* be okay. You'll be fine."

I almost said, I'm not here for you. At least, not in the way almost everything else on her campus was there for her. I *could* be there for her. How many books had I read in my life about characters completely different from me culturally and historically that I'd still managed to learn from, even enjoy? And in this case, my novel was about a young woman experiencing her first year of college, being read by someone experiencing her first year of college, but this young woman hadn't seen herself in my narrator because my narrator was not white like her. That fact says more about the failure of both her imagination and America's dominant culture than it does about the merits of fiction. She could choose to look for commonality, the same way those of us whose experiences aren't centered in our educational systems do every day, as a matter of course, as a strategy for survival—but that choice was hers to make, not mine. Her response to my comments proved that she didn't know how much she needed me, and if her college never required her to take a class where these issues could be carefully and compassionately explored, she might never know. And in that moment, that was fine. I was there for a version of me that needed to see a fellow Latinx woman call out an ugly truth and keep going in the face of it. I decided the Q&A was over, thanked the crowd, and left the stage.

She remained seated in the front row, friends consoling her. I resisted the pull to walk up to her, squat down, engage her even more. I ignored the tears of this one white woman the way we all should ignore them when much more is at stake and turned instead to the group of four women of color and two white women who'd materialized near the front of the stage, students who mattered just as much, each of them clutching my novel—about a girl a lot like them, doing exactly what they were doing—across their chests as if it were a new kind of armor.

My armor in college had been Maxine Hong Kingston's *The Woman Warrior*. To hear a version of what was happening to me in college happening to the narrator of Kingston's novel-memoir gave me the courage to keep going. The epigraph of my novel comes from that one. To have written a book that could do the same for other people—I can't put into words what this means to me. I can only describe the sensation, which is one of filling up inside that rises past my heart and into my throat, wrecking my ability to talk.

■

Is it uncomfortable, reading all this? Does your answer depend on your race, on whether or not you consider yourself white? Are you feeling like that white girl in the crowd who wanted to tell me about reverse racism? If you do consider yourself white and don't feel like that girl, are you not yet uncomfortable because, despite this being about your people, you don't think it's about *your* people? Because, as a white person, you've gotten to be just you your whole life?

The concept of standing in for a whole category of humans wasn't forced on me until college, when white professors and white students alike would ask me not my opinion, but the opinion of people like me—*where does your community stand on this?* And because these moments were some of the few times people acknowledged that I was even in the room, I would answer as the official Latinx ambassador, thinking I had the right, because I'd been made to feel I had the right by the people in charge of the space we then inhabited. This unintentional act of bigotry has a name: It's called *spotlighting*, though I didn't know that when I gave this experience over to the narrator of my novel. I have it happen to her and watch her endure it. Then I endure it again, when white students read this section and ask me, as a visitor on their campus, "But why is that bad? Why is it wrong to ask her what other Cubans think?" Whereas the students of color tell me, almost laughing, "Oh my god, this happens to me *all the time.*"

I sometimes ask white students in my classes (and they are full, mostly, of white students) what white people think of certain things—about legalizing marijuana, for instance, or the current president. Every time I've tried this, the very first thing every student does is laugh.

To them, it's a funny premise: that all white people could possibly have the same opinion about anything. If they protest or seem appropriately baffled, I say what I've been told when put in the same situation, *Right, right, I know, but just* generally *what do white people think about legalizing weed/ the president? Like, in general?* They never know what to say. They can't even understand the question. Obviously, they reason, I am insane.

■

When it came to having the privilege of choosing a career path, I did what people who've internalized systemic oppression sometimes do: I aimed for something different that felt more *appropriate*, more *attainable*. I decided I'd make a good high school English teacher. I'd still get to talk about books and teach people to love and value the act of writing. And I'd have summers to work on all the novels and short stories I wanted to write.

Then something happened that very subtly set me on a different path. No, it's not the typical "I found the right mentor who guided me" story, though I did end up finding an invaluable mentor, a Latina professor—the only one in creative writing at my college at the time—who guided me and my work in countless ways. (My college professor count, by the way: one.) She was not the one who nudged me down the professorial road, though she did give me the tools to find it and keep on it.

No, what happened was I stayed up too late one night in the dorm, and I went in on pizza with some girls on my floor, something I normally didn't do because, based on my budget, pizza was a splurge. But this night, as we crammed for finals, we got to talking about what we were hoping to do with our lives. It was maybe one thirty in the morning; we were all bleary from studying and stress and sleep deprivation.

Of the four other women in the room, three of them had at least one parent who was a lawyer. (Most of my fellow students were from affluent families—even now, I have to stop myself from saying I had no business being there, but that's how it felt for me, most of my time there.) These three women— the daughters of the lawyers—each said that worse comes to worst, they too would be lawyers. The woman who did not have at least one lawyer as a parent (she told us her father was an "analyst" and left it at that) also said she wanted to be a lawyer. A tax attorney, she clarified, but she hoped to also own an art gallery. To me this made her seem more interesting than the others, and I remember thinking we'd stay friends.

I was quiet during this whole exchange, listening for clues as to what I should say when the question inevitably came my way. I was searching my brain for what they would consider the right answer, which I somehow intuited was not high school English teacher. When they asked me, I blurted out what I thought was an appropriately upgraded version of my dream, "I want to be an English professor."

And the minute I said it, I knew it could be true. Granted, I didn't have a completely accurate picture of what that entailed. I had taken three English classes by then, and I thought English professors were people who got to read and write books all day, have deep thoughts about said books, then share those thoughts with an adoring audience. And granted, I genuinely did not think I was smart enough to be a professor. Even today, when I think of a professor, the image that comes to my mind is of a specific white man, Dr. James Adams, a scholar of Victorian literature who wore a for-real tweed jacket—with the elbow patches and everything—and who was so freaky smart and accomplished that I remember tracing my fingers over the written comments he'd pen at the end of my papers, hoping his brilliance would transfer over to me that way somehow. But I knew when the sentence came out of my mouth that I wanted to be someone who made knowledge, who got to live in books and in theories about books, who got to spend her life writing while teaching future generations of writers how to hone their craft, how to pick apart the books they loved and discover how they were built.

So yeah, that night in the dorms, I said *English professor* and awaited their verdict.

One girl said, "Well, I guess they make OK money."

"What's *okay money*?" I asked. Bold, for me, because money was something that didn't get brought up so directly in social situations. My parents' reported combined income that year was around forty thousand dollars. I remember this because we'd filled out the FAFSA together, and I figured going to college would help me come close to that number on my own, which meant I could have a good life doing what I loved while still paying my bills.

"I think they make, like, at a private school? Eighty thousand maybe? Like I said, not great but OK."

Now, she overshot that number big-time, especially when you take into account that this was the year 2000. And she was likely quoting a full professor's salary. But she said it with authority, so I believed her.

I was floored by two things. One, this salary was "OK money" to someone like her. And two, even if she was off by a factor of two, my dream job paid more—possibly much more—than what my parents together typically earned. And while it would still take me far too long to believe I was really and truly professor material, those girls nodding their heads at my non-lawyer career choice—their approval—echoed the *Yes!* that had suddenly materialized in my own heart.

■

I went after my first tenure-track job with a ferocity that barely made sense. I knew I wanted that job as much as I'd ever wanted anything. I recognized it as the life I'd wanted but that I'd convinced myself over time was not really a possibility. Still, I would never have even applied for it had I not heard directly from someone on the search committee saying they'd read my work and would be interested in seeing an application from me. I would never have thought myself qualified enough without that small encouragement.

And I would never have been able to put together a successful application without asking for tons and tons of help from people who'd been through the process. It was something that was hard for me to do—asking for help—but it was absolutely crucial to overcoming the gaps I had in my knowledge when it came to "the market" and all its nuances. The Latina professor I mentioned earlier, the writer Helena María Viramontes, worked much harder than she had to with me the first time I went on the job market, especially considering that I hadn't been her student for close to a decade by then. But that's what I wanted to be for someone else, what I wanted to strive for. My vision of a professor had changed enough to include someone like me: someone without a tweed jacket, a writer first whose love and respect for the craft of writing fuels her commitment to teaching it to others.

With every class I teach or story I write or talk I prepare, I'm still becoming a professor. I still think, when I'm getting dressed to teach or for a meeting, *I'm putting on my professor costume.* It still sometimes feels like an act that I can't admit is my reality.

I suspect I'll feel this way all my life.

■

I earned tenure last year. I'm proud of the accomplishment, but it didn't mean everything I thought it would mean to me, and I know it's because of the roundabout way I came to working in academia. The real job, the career, is being a writer; that's the path I was even more afraid to let myself want.

The moment I held a hardcopy of my novel in my hands for the first time, I wept, alone in my kitchen, because it hit me that I honestly thought that moment would never come. I had doubted that novel would ever exist to such an extent that I couldn't believe I now held it in my hands. I still feel that way. Sometimes someone will catch me inside this feeling when I'm signing books. I look up to find them with a book I wrote in their hands, opening it up for me to sign, and I almost blurt out, *where did you get that?* I'm not sure if this feeling will ever go away, either, and in this case I'm not sure that I want it to, because the moment of realizing that it's true—that I'd really accomplished this thing that for so long I'd worked for—fills me to bursting every time. Earning tenure was important and valuable and meaningful and not at all like that moment where I slid my novel out from a slightly beat-up padded envelope for the first time.

■

When I worked for a nonprofit organization as a college access counselor, I constantly felt like I was learning from my students, from every single one of them. And I never doubted that my work was making a positive difference in this country. But because of what that job demanded of my time and my emotions, I *did* doubt whether I would ever write another book if I continued to work there. I tell myself being a professor is the best of both worlds, but maybe what I really mean to say is it's a trade-off.

I don't know if I'll be a professor forever. There's more to the machine of it than I anticipated, and depending on the class, the audience with which I'm sharing my thoughts on writing and books isn't always adoring. I sometimes joke that maybe I need a tweed jacket. I sometimes dream of quitting to open the hair salon I'd wanted to run when I was little, or to go to dental school. I have occasionally indulged in drafting resignation letters: "Thank you for the tenure, however, I am leaving academia to be a tugboat captain/florist." But the fact that I'm somewhat ambivalent about my day job is what makes me good at it. I teach as if I have nothing to lose, which helps me tell my students the truth—about why the faces in the room are mostly a certain color, or how we are all part of an oppressive structure perpetuating all sorts of bigotry just by sitting in that room. I don't believe these institutions will figure out a way to solve their own problems. They were designed to do the opposite. When I speak at other predominantly white campuses, I've reminded the students of color and the women about this fact: This place never imagined you here, and your exclusion was a fundamental premise in its initial design. I push students toward protest, toward using their understandable and justified rage to be heard, to literally and metaphorically burn things down. Then I come back to my own campus and sit in my office and listen to the lights buzz overheard while thanking the universe that, for now, I have health insurance.

The contradiction makes me sick. And the only thing that eases the nausea is the writing.

The writing asks you to question the job.

The job lets me afford the writing.

The job is why you're reading this.

A PROGNOSIS

N LATE NOVEMBER 2015, I HEADED HOME FOR the Miami Book Fair to promote my first novel, which had been out since August. A hometown reading meant my parents would be in the crowd, a weird combination of pride and distress splayed across their faces. I'd launched the book in Miami, and at that event, after I'd read aloud from the opening chapter, my father, without warning and from his spot in the crowd, announced to everyone there that the parents the book described were not at all based on him and my mom. People laughed, and so did I, though I know he hadn't said it to be funny: The reading he'd just heard was his first glimpse into what the book was about.

This time, before the Miami Book Fair event, he told me I should make a similar disclaimer. Leading up to that afternoon, his stomach had been reeling. He hadn't managed to keep any real food down for days, and he was running to the bathroom so often that I worried he wouldn't make it through the reading. His whole digestive tract was rebelling against him, and apparently so was I. Minutes before the event began, as I made polite banter with another writer, he snared the back of my arm and directed me toward the venue's doors, saying nothing until we were outside. He turned me to face him and, now gripping my shoulder, explained what he thought I should do—to "help people understand," as he put it. I told him there was no way I could make such a disclaimer. I'd been raised to accommodate his demands, so this was not the response he'd anticipated. He released my shoulder and I fumbled through an explanation of how a disclaimer like that was unprofessional and unnecessary, as everyone in the crowd understood that a novel is a work of fiction. I remember feeling outside of myself as I spoke—my hands going numb, then tingling—hoping that the people hovering near the doors wouldn't hear whatever he said next. I knew he'd dismiss my reasons; I knew he'd be angry; I just hoped he would keep his voice down. He cut off my explanation and backed away from me, saying, too loud, "You know what? Do whatever you want," and then he charged back into the event space. I eventually followed, taking my place on stage. And then, as I began to read from my work, I accidentally made eye contact with him when I leaned forward into the microphone. He looked so sick and pale—not the tight-jawed face I'd expected, but still instinctually frightening—that I blurted out some nonsense about how my dad never dumped garbage into a canal the way the father does in my novel's opening.

Except that's not true: In real life, he absolutely dumped garbage in the canal across the street from our house. I borrowed this detail from reality and loaned it to Ricky, the father in my novel. My father's name is Rey.

He hadn't read my first book and had no plans to read this next one. I suspect he was afraid of what he might find, but his stated excuse had always been that he was too busy, that his work as an electrical inspector left him too drained to read, and he stocked his weekends with overtime. When was he supposed to go through *all those pages?*

He always joked, "I'll wait for the movie." He always said, after attending any reading I gave, that he'd already heard enough.

■

For everyone in my immediate family, stress manifests itself in our digestive tracts, though for most everyone else—my mother, sister, grandmother—the trouble (when it comes) is at the back end. My system has it upside down; I tend to throw up when stressed, like a human version of a sea cucumber. It happened predictably enough that I'd even given it a cute name: The Crucet Curse. It was so much a part of who I'd become that throwing up when something nerve-racking approached was (to those who know and love me) just that weird thing Jennine did. And up until Americans made a sexual predator our president, I was able to write it off as only mildly inconvenient.

The throwing up originated one night late in high school, during a date that went very badly. Me-Today thinks back to this night—the dimly lit booth, the spiral-bound menus spread open between us, the cloud of cologne wafting across the table—and wants to grab Me-Then by her too-boney shoulder and say, *Let's get the fuck out of here, this is going to get much worse.* But I know that girl wouldn't move. I know Me-Then would think Me-Today is very weird, living far from the ocean and convinced she must wear tights under every dress to feel safe. Me-Then would be shocked that Me-Today hasn't produced any children. Me-Then would have harsh things to say about the state of Me-Today's hair. But ever since that night and the traumas for which it paved the way, my body has responded to certain anxieties with an almost comical reaction: Like Stan Marsh in *South Park* every time Wendy walks by, I barf.

It used to just be things that made sense. I barfed before

every exam in college, before every show in which I performed as a sketch comedian. But then I starting throwing up before I had to *administer* an exam, sympathy-barfing on behalf of my students. I threw up when tax documents showed up in the mail. I threw up when forced to make phone calls. I always know when it needs to happen and I always, always feel better after.

Between hurls, I usually say, without thinking about it, *I hate this,* or *I hate myself.* And sometimes, my body goes back to that night where my mind won't go. Then it's, *I hate you.*

■

A week after the Miami Book Fair, I was back in Lincoln to finish out my first semester of teaching at my new job. I taught at night that term, and on my walks home, I'd often cut through the lobby of a hotel. So it was in a painfully outdated Embassy Suites that I got the call every person dreads: My mom had driven my father to the emergency room after he'd passed out while sweeping the driveway. (He's the kind of man who sweeps his driveway.) They hadn't gone to the ER right away. He'd waited until later that night, after a light rain had fallen on his face as he lay on the concrete, and after he stood back up and finished the sweeping. While his stomach troubles hadn't gone away after my reading, he's the kind of man who blames something like passing out on either having had too much coffee or not enough coffee. He often forgot to eat while he was working, never registering until it was way too late that he even felt hunger. I have the same bad habit, lack the same ability to recognize what my body is telling me it needs.

It was my father who called me to deliver the news, which was strange. We hardly ever spoke on the phone, as my mom typically did the work of relating anything interesting I said to him, and vice versa. It had always been this way, even in college, and even before that; she was his interpreter, reminding us that he loved us even if he couldn't show it in ways we understood or needed, teaching us to read his moods for signs of volatility. Every story I know about my father's traumatic upbringing I only know because my mother told it to me, usually as an excuse for whatever distant and hurtful treatment he was enacting against us. She deployed these stories to defend him, and to teach us to be thankful that he wasn't worse.

My father then explained that the passing out was just the beginning of the story; within hours of being admitted to the emergency room, doctors told him he had advanced leukemia. They told him that without treatment he had about six weeks to live. He was fifty-eight.

I flew home a day later, arriving a couple of hours before the start of his first chemotherapy treatment. He'd decided to undergo it—of course he did. He told anyone who asked that he felt fine, that he was actually totally healthy aside from the cancer thing. He bragged that he had never taken a sick day from work in his life. One doctor coaxed my mother and sister and me out of his room in order to warn us that my father would be receiving "the strongest chemotherapy on the planet." He and the nurses gave us a rundown of what treatment would look like, how crucial it would be for my father to keep physical contact with us and visitors to a minimum because the risk of infection once treatment was underway would be the biggest threat. My sister laughed that this wouldn't be hard, blurting out, "We never touch him, he hates being touched." *Whatever*, I thought, these doctors don't know Rey like we know him. He is tough, even mean. Chemotherapy should be afraid of *him*.

We were told that, best-case scenario, he'd be in the hospital for four weeks. "I'll be out by Christmas," my dad said.

Despite the doctor trying to warn us of what could and would come, we were so optimistic that our main worry was how we were going to keep my father entertained over the duration of his hospital stay. This was my father's biggest worry as well. "I have no excuse now, do I?" he said to me just as this all started, weeks before he would end up on a ventilator and on dialysis, machines doing the work his lungs and kidneys couldn't do. "I gotta read your books now, don't I?" He didn't mean *because I might die*. He meant: because the time and work excuses no longer held. In his mind, he was about to have more time than he could handle.

I was surprised my books were even on his mind in that moment, but the double whammy of him having cancer and him admitting he would have to read my work made me think, *Finally! We will finally learn to talk to each other and he will no longer be this cold mystery to me. This is actually going to be great once we come out on the other side. This will change everything.* I decided this was the kind of positive thinking the doctors were encouraging us to have. The doctors also encouraged us to make the room feel like home, since it would be weeks before he'd be allowed to leave it. As he dictated from the bed, we made a list of the things he wanted us to bring from home. My books were on it, in my mother's handwriting. While unpacking, my dad placed both books on the nightstand by his hospital bed. He said he would wait until he got "really bored" to start them.

Very soon after that, things got much worse, and so he never read them. That makes it sound like he died, but that's not what happened (though he almost died several times). In fact, as of this writing, he is in remission. He never read my work because, ultimately, he just couldn't, for reasons he won't ever explain to me, for reasons he himself will not face.

Reasons that will probably haunt every book I ever write.

■

When I was a little girl, my mother and grandmother often sat me on the kitchen counter and made me drink Malta soda with condensed milk stirred into it, high-calorie stuff meant to fatten me up. Engórdate, they commanded. It didn't work. I drank and drank, developed a love for the stuff—the way the sugar coated my teeth, how the carbonation, weighed down by all that sweet milk, turned the soda silky—but once inside, it never took. I couldn't make my body do what they wanted.

As a girl on that date years later, the guy who'd brought me to the Cheesecake Factory—the nice one in Coconut Grove with the jacked-up prices—let me order that fucking straw-berry lemonade and whatever I wanted for dinner. As the waitress turned away with our dessert orders, the guy leaned over the table and gave me those words—*I let you order that fucking strawberry lemonade and whatever you wanted for dinner*—and then he laughed. I remember my freshly shaved armpits suddenly stinging at the sound. In the midst of what-ever he found funny, he said, "Don't worry, it'll cost you later."

I did and didn't know what he meant. I was sixteen. Maybe he was kidding. He was nineteen. I excused myself and went to the bathroom, my head down to watch my steps—I was wearing heels.

I pushed with my whole body against the door, and once it swung closed behind me, sealing me off from the clatter of the dining room, I leaned over the sink to look in the mirror—too much eyeliner, too much blush—and asked myself, *Do you want this?* My body knew its answer immediately. A forceful no: I threw up in the sink, my inaugural stress vomit.

My mind, too, said no. While rinsing my mouth, I tried to figure out a way to get home that wouldn't embarrass anyone. This was before teenagers carried cell phones. And this was in Miami, where public transportation left (and still leaves) much to be desired. My mind worked and worked to figure out a way to keep my body safe. My mother had warned me the night before that good Cuban girls always go out with chaperones, but fine, okay, she would tell my dad I was going out with friends because this guy did seem so nice and he was so handsome and he came into our house and looked my mother in the eye and she knew then he'd never hurt me. Besides, God would protect me. Besides, she knew this guy's mother. My mind was trying to make sense of the guy she'd met with the guy I was about to meet.

As I ran water in the sink and used paper towels to pick up chunks too large for the drain, my body somehow already knew it would need to go to extremes to keep me safe. And that it would fail. The mind let the body down and made it do something it didn't want to do.

I ignored what the body told me for a long time after that. It did cost me later, and it kept costing me, until I couldn't afford it anymore.

■

I can say with confidence that literature has never brought my father comfort (it was, after all, my mom who took me to the library, my mom who taught me how to read in the first place). I've yet to see him read a book that wasn't filled with the latest electrical codes or glossy pictures of cars, so perhaps it was misguided of me to hope that he'd read the books I'd written and take some sort of comfort from them. Because the only thing I've ever seen bring my father comfort is work. When his kidneys were failing post-chemo and the high nitrogen and carbon dioxide levels in his blood began to impact his brain function, he kept hallucinating that he was pressing buttons on an iPad, trying to submit inspection reports. While in that state, he repeatedly and feverishly warned us about a failed fire inspection, saying that there were problems with the ceiling tiles, that the building was unsafe. One of the last things he said to me before becoming unresponsive was that he needed me to "hit the REFRESH button," swearing as he thrashed in his bed, "It's not up to code!"

"He's going to a place where he feels confident," the psychologist assigned to our family told us the day before my father had to be placed on a ventilator. "It's the brain's way of trying to take back control." I couldn't believe it. Even in his delirium, even as he slipped closer to the possible end of his life, instead of reaching for us, my father was going to work.

Our psychologist had his work cut out for him. My father was in complete denial that he needed a psychologist's help, despite his first-day-of-chemo pronouncement that "Half this shit is attitude." He told us not to talk to the psychologist lest we be labeled crazy. He warned that they kept a record of everything you said. When the doctor would ask my dad about his feelings, he'd answer with aggressively short sentences: "I'm fine," or "I'm good." Of the four of us, I'm the only one who'd been to a therapist (years earlier, while in graduate school, and again when my marriage was ending), which means I was the first to break rank when my father's condi-tion dramatically deteriorated seven days into treatment. I followed the psychologist out of the room after another brief, awkward check-in and told him everything: how my father had told us not to talk to him; how my mother refused to leave his side to the point of making herself ill; how she often seemed hysterical and no longer trusted the nurses to do their jobs; how my father yelled in his sleep, saying things like "Get ahold of yourself, asshole!" and "I should've died already" and "I'm not really here." I showed the doctor the notebook I was keeping where I was documenting everything as it happened, told him I was a writer. He then said he'd recognized our last name, had seen it on a book his wife was reading and would be teaching the next semester—she was, like me, a profes-sor. His recognition in that context felt surreal, a reminder of some life I'd lived that was over, and now my life was the on-cology wing of this hospital and nothing else, then or ever. He handed me his business card (the psychologist ended every interaction by handing me his business card; this happened enough times that I suspected he was earning rewards points for every card he gave out) and told me he'd check in with us again in the evening.

I went back in the room after having been gone for long enough that it was obvious I'd said a lot to the psychologist. No one was talking. I could guess what my parents were thinking, so I said, "His job is to help us get through this. He can't do that if we don't talk to him."

Only my father responded. He said, "All your intelligence flies out the window when you come into this room."

I wrote that sentence down, too.

■

The first time I told my mom I was seeing a therapist, while still in graduate school, she said exactly what I thought she'd say, because it was a refrain that had kept me from seeking out help for more than a year: "But you're not crazy." She said, "You just need more sun, more exercise, you don't eat right." She said, "Therapy is for Americans." By which she meant—because we are, in fact, Americans—for white people. The narrator of *The Mambo Kings Play Songs of Love*, the Pulitzer Prize–winning novel by Oscar Hijuelos, has this to say about Cubans and mental health: "Cubans then (and Cubans now) didn't know about psychological problems. Cubans who felt bad went to their friends, ate and drank and went out dancing. Most of the time they wouldn't think about their problems. A psychological problem was part of someone's character."

Cubans then *and* Cubans now. The first time I read this passage, I felt sick with recognition. A whole group of new Americans—all having suffered the trauma of exile, many of them as children—minimizing what had happened to them as problems they could eat and drink and dance away. A psychological problem as part of someone's character: So my father was not practicing avoidance; he was just a workaholic. And so was I. And my character was just too sensitive, my father's just too angry and distant. It's just who we are—so says Hijuelos's narrator, so says my mother—and not a thing to work through.

The second time I started seeing a therapist, when I sensed the impending end of my marriage, I kept it to myself. I told my parents about my divorce a week after filing for it.

When I returned to Lincoln (exactly two days after my father was discharged from the hospital, on the eve of classes beginning again), I started seeing a therapist to help me dismantle the system of avoidance disguised as productivity that had, for so long, kept both of us working. The process would mean accepting what had happened to me years earlier— events that began with that dinner, events I still cannot name for what they were even now as I write this sentence. But I'd just witnessed the places avoidance led and its limits, and there would be more lessons to come.

■

At the end of May 2016, my family spent a week together at the beach, an impromptu celebration with the stated aim of helping us all relax after everything we'd been through. We booked it before we'd even gotten the results from my father's biopsy. Cancer-free or not, my dad planned to go back to work at the beginning of June, so if we were going to schedule some family time, he said it had to be before his return date.

During the trip, my mother, sister, and I couldn't help

talking about our weeks in the hospital, recounting what we'd experienced, filling in gaps and questioning each other's memory of the endless hours we spent sitting by him. Many of those days, my father doesn't remember because he was heavily sedated, and I could sense the terror in him when we'd bring these days up. "Stop talking about that," he said more than once over his shoulder, his face determinedly pointed at the ocean. "I don't want to hear about that. Forget it happened."

One night during this trip, sitting around the dining table over pizza, I got brave enough to ask him what he planned on changing about his life now that he was healthy. Back in the hospital, on his third day of chemo, I'd asked him a similar question after he'd said out of nowhere, "Once I'm outta here, it's a whole new attitude." I'd asked, "How would you change?" and he was quiet for a long moment before saying, "Treat you guys a little better." I wanted to know if he remembered that, if he had other things on his list now that it seemed the worst was behind him. It was a question I'd started asking myself: What would I let my body teach me?

"I'm not healthy," he corrected. "I have to get tested again in three months."

Because one of the things I wanted to change about my life was my fear of his anger and the way he used it to keep his distance from us, I pressed on. "Okay, fine, let's go with that. Let's say in three months when you get tested, the cancer is back. What are you gonna do with the next three months, before you go into the hospital for more treatment?"

He looked away from us and said, all his patience gone, "Worry about having cancer again, Jennine."

I didn't know what to say back to him. I felt disappointment flood me—a profound, body-filling sadness, an exhausted sadness that I now recognize as the hallmark of my relationship with my father, a defining characteristic I'm still working to accept rather than fix—because what he was telling me with this answer was that nothing would change.

Because my father (and my mother, by example) trained us well in the art of deflecting and covering for the discomfort he induces with his callousness, I quickly posed the question to my sister: "What about you, you have three months to *really* live—what would you do with it?"

"I don't know," she said. "Watch TV? I'd probably just watch TV."

"Are you serious?" I pressed my fingers to the bridge of my nose. She was twelve weeks pregnant with her first child.

My mom spoke up then. "I would go to Spain. I have always wanted to go there."

"Spain is really cool, I *love* Spain," my sister said. Of the four of us, she's the only one who's been there, and she tends to remind us of this fact whenever that country comes up in conversation.

"Wait, you guys *should* go to Spain!" I said. "You should go, like, tomorrow."

My father leaned forward and rubbed his hands over his whole face and head, his palms scrubbing the hair that was already growing back—a more exaggerated, exasperated version of the gesture I'd just made.

My mom asked me, "What about you?"

Three months felt like nothing, and without warning and before I could articulate an answer, I started to cry—I thought of the books I would never write, the literature I would never create.

"What?" my mom said, laughing sweetly at my sudden tears.

"I'm sorry," I said. "I just thought about how there's no way I could finish writing a novel in three months, and even if I could, there's no way I'd get to see it out in the world."

Literature might never have been a comfort for my father, but it had meant so much to me that I'd devoted my life to making it myself. I don't see the act of writing as a form of therapy, but I do think that what you write will reveal things you didn't consciously recognize as feelings you held, expose beliefs you didn't know you had. Like how halfway through writing the previous sentence, I felt the need to switch to the direct address instead of using *I*: a switch that illustrates my own struggle to accept that my writing can reveal my darkest feelings about people I love, that the difficult family at the center of my novel came from a place I couldn't yet consciously visit. Writing fiction is my work, my form of artful avoidance that always inevitably leads me right back to the heart of the thing I am avoiding.

My mom leaned away from the table and said, "You're

crying like that about *work*? You wouldn't spend those three months with your *family*?" I didn't think about the implications of her response, of who she might really be talking to. I didn't think about how in my novel, the father character remains a mystery to his wife and children because of his own childhood experiences (the abuse and neglect he suffered at the hands of an alcoholic father and an agoraphobic, unloving mother, each of them also survivors of unspeakable traumas), how those experiences prevent the father from engaging with the daughters he watched his wife raise. I thought only, *I am my father's daughter.*

I sputtered back, defensive as usual, "Uh, *none of us* said family, *you* didn't say family, did you?" My dad stood up from the table and took his pizza slice to the couch to watch TV, letting out a big burp followed by, "Whatever."

At the end of his third week back at work, he was already taking on overtime. He goes in on Saturdays. If he talks to my mom about his pain—if he's still in pain—I don't know about it; I live in another state now, and my work has taken me far from home.

■

Very shortly after the 2016 election and months into my work with a therapist, I found myself standing in my home office, yelling at my body out of nowhere. The familiar sensations that normally told me I was about to throw up had started happening much more often, when I wasn't about to do something important. I felt like throwing up at the simplest of tasks, tasks that for so long had served me well enough as productive distractions. This time it was emails. I was angry that I seemed to suddenly be getting worse, not better. Through a clenched jaw I didn't register until moments later, I told my body that if it kept this up I would end it. *I will end you*, I spat at my fists, ready to hit myself the way my attacker had hit me, and I meant it so much that I started crying, beating those fists on my thighs and saying, *I hate you, I hate you.*

Get ahold of yourself, asshole.

In the months since my dad left the hospital, I'd been working slowly to face events that I'd long refused to admit even happened. I was listening to my body in ways I hadn't in a long time. And then an older, cartoonish version of the *you* who sometimes snuck out between my retches won the presidency. Americans elected a man who bragged about assaulting women, and their acceptance of his actions sent my body this message: *We are not safe.* The Crucet Curse stopped being something I could give a cute name. My body's rebellion against my avoidance escalated dramatically, and would keep escalating if I kept trying to suppress it. My body revolted until I accepted that its unruliness was the very thing that would save me.

For too long, I believed the lies my mind invented, lies originating in popular culture: *This was not a big deal, it was your own fault anyway, it didn't even matter, it doesn't matter. Your people have gone through worse—your parents left a*

*country behind. Your dad is battling cancer. He almost died.
Your pain is nothing. You got off easy. So you throw up sometimes. No one has to know. That's nothing. Look at how* stable
*you are. Look at the books you've made, the worlds you've built
in your fiction, aren't they proof that what happened wasn't so
bad? That what happened isn't even worth telling?*

But my body knew better, had for years tried to disrupt
this dangerous narrative in the most grotesque way it could.
In the wake of the election, my body had made work impossible. It had taken away the best distraction I'd ever had. What,
in its absence, could I make?

■

When our time in the hospital started, while my dad was still
relatively well and before the effects of chemo had floored him
entirely, I found myself trying to keep us all entertained with
a personality quiz. I'd dubbed myself the activities director
on the Cancer Cruise Ship, coming up with annoying shit for
my family do every day to keep the TV from becoming everything. Reading from the list of questions, I asked my father
what three things he was better at than most people.

His first, immediate answer: Driving.

After a little thought, he gave us his second answer, "Fix-
ing almost anything."

"That's true," my mom half-whispered, not wanting to
interrupt, as it was a rare thing that he was willing to go
along with the quiz; he typically dismissed things like this

as stupid and would leave the room, except now, he couldn't. "Remember that time he fixed the dryer after that rat got stuck in the drum?"

His third answer, on the heels of my mom's comment: "Holding my feelings in—no, keeping my emotions—putting them into work, putting them there."

My sister and I tried to hide our surprise at how plainly he'd stated this, at the fact that he saw the element of his personality that had kept us most apart as a strength. My mom nodded, not surprised at all. And because much of my profession is devoted to the opposite of this—to using writing to unearth and investigate deeper truths that my dad would rather keep private (and from my sister and me, even secret)—I wrote all of this down as precisely as I could, the way I would come to write down everything that happened over the next few weeks, pages I continue to write, pages I need to write, pages he should never make himself read.

■

Our bodies have a lot to teach us. I'm still learning, week by week, to listen to mine and to accept and trust what it tells me. I haven't thrown up as a response to stress in a while, though the behavior got worse before it got any better—my therapist warned me this was the case for lots of people. Sometimes the work of therapy asks me to write about events that still cause my mouth to fill with spit and send me running to a toilet. I always saw writing as a way of protecting myself from those events, not as a way of teaching my body to accept that those events are in my past. Writing felt too powerful and sacred a tool. I resisted using it until I realized that its power was exactly what my body deserved.

It's a tool I wish I could loan my father in much the same way I wish he'd read the books I write for him—because through all this work and from everything I've come to accept about our relationship, I have also come to accept that my books are in fact for him, and for people like him—people like me. This will always be true, whether he reads them or not: I want each book I write to be a way into something we couldn't otherwise face.

I'm writing a new novel about a man who calls Miami home, and that's all I'm okay saying about it for now. I'm protective of my characters. As I write, I see the world he's building—that I'm building, through him—and it's a place that pulls me back in each day. I want to see what we'll make of it. I want us to keep building. I don't yet know what to hope for. So far, the character is like no one I've ever met, and yet I know him. I'm eager to see what the story might, in time, show us all.

ACKNOWLEDGMENTS

Many thanks to my extraordinary agent, Adam Eaglin, whose guidance and resilience I am grateful for every single day. Thanks to everyone at the Cheney Agency, especially Isabel Mendía, for their tireless work.

My immense gratitude to Anna deVries, whose expert editorial vision and brilliance made this book so much stronger (and whose daughter has the best name). Thanks, too, to Stephen M. Morrison, James Meader, Sara DeLozier, Darin Keesler, Kolt Beringer, Cecilia Molinari, and the whole Picador team for their enthusiasm, hard work, and support. A special thank you to Byron Echeverria for willing this book into existence (and for his friendship), and to Caroline Casey for helping all things grow.

My eternal thanks to Rachel Dry, my editor at *The New York Times*, for emailing me out of the blue in 2015 and thus inadvertently getting this whole project started. I am forever indebted to you for your persistence, your patience, and your faith in my voice: Thank you for always finding what I meant to say. A debt of gratitude also to Roxane Gay for publishing my nonfiction in *Medium* and *Gay Magazine* (and for her encouragement to fight for what I wanted); and to Curtis Sittenfeld, for everything, but most recently: for taking notes in St. Louis and giving them to me later with the promise that there was a book in there somewhere.

Thank you to my colleagues at the University of Nebraska in the Department of English and the Institute for Ethnic Studies for our lively and honest conversations, and for the vital resources—time, space, and support—to complete this book. For "proudly serving misfits since 2011," thank you to The Bay, where much of this book was drafted and discussed. Thank you to Gina Furr, Maggie Bertsche, Cait Cain: This book would not exist without your help, your talents, and your expertise.

Much gratitude to my writerly siblings, Stacey Waite and Xhenet Aliu, for their generous feedback on the messes that became essays in this book. Thank you to Hope Wabuke, who in her very existence is a reminder of warmer, more loving climates, and whose generosity and care with this manuscript pushed me to live up to her brilliance.

To the students enrolled in our magical Fall 2017 English 352 workshop: Thank you for letting me practice what I preach and for becoming a family. Thanks to Lana Lobsiger Flagtwet, for her example, and to Mary Ryan, for helping me find home. Many thanks, too, to the colleges and universities whose invitations to come speak about *Make Your Home Among Strangers* with their students provoked my thinking about questions that led to more questions, which eventually led to these essays.

Mil gracias to Margarita and Fabio Nodarse, for giving me a piece of your heart, for feeding me in more ways than one, and for taking me in.

Thank you to my wonderful parents, Maria and Rey (I promise the next book so far doesn't have any parents in it at all); to my sister and her husband, Kathy and Jorge Villavicencio; and to my amazing niece, Paloma, aka the Great Gertrude aka Bistec Palomilla aka Lil PP aka our future volcanologist/sandhill crane expert. I can't wait to see what names you will someday reject and embrace.

And finally, to Alejandro Nodarse, my favorite human on the planet, for lovingly bringing me back to the page again and again. This book—like the others, before I could even know—is for you.